THE COVID-19 PANDEMIC

CHALLANGES, ISSUES AND OUTBREAK FOR INNOVATION

MR. KRITTIBAS DATTA DR. MUKTA GOYAL

Contents

Foreword

It gives me great pleasure to announce the publication of "The Covid-19 Pandemic: Challenges, Issues, and Outbreak for Innovation," edited by Mr. Krittibas Datta and Dr.Mukta Goyal. This book focuses on the Issues and Challenges of the COVID-19 Pandemic in India, as well as the Outbreak for Innovation. Both the editors, who have worked as professionals and are also experienced faculty members, discuss the various issues and challenges of the Covid-19 pandemic in this remarkable publication, as directed by their research and hard work. I want to congratulate them both on this outstanding accomplishment, which is the result of their tireless efforts. Finally, I would like to state that the current volume will assist future generations in providing a variety of knowledge.

Prof. (Dr.) Narendra Sharma

Vice-Chancellor

Motherhood University, Roorkee

Preface

When Covid-19 struck, it compelled societal changes all over the world. Nearly overnight, governments issued orders restricting large crowds, limiting in-person business operations, and encouraging people to work from home as much as possible. As a result, businesses and schools alike began to look for ways to operate remotely, thanks to the internet. They used various collaboration platforms and video conferencing capabilities to stay in touch with colleagues, clients, and students while working from home offices.

This pandemic has created an unprecedented demand for digital health technology solutions, revealing successful solutions such as population screening, infection tracking, prioritising resource use and allocation, and designing targeted responses. In different parts of the world, the socio-economic and educational system is facing some of its biggest trials yet, from the COVID-19 pandemic. The continuous closing of Schools and Colleges has vibrated the entire education system.

India's effort to combat COVID-19 virus with vaccinated policy has been praised over the globe. However, the lockdown came with an economic cost and cascading impact on all the sections of society. During this conditions emerging technologies such as Artificial Intelligence (AI) aid in the development of vaccines, predicting which public health measures will be most effective, and keeping the public informed of scientific developments. They have also enabled us to move much of our lives online, keeping economic and educational systems running when most people are at home and keeping us connected to one another.

However, not all regions and social groups are equally capable of harnessing the power of digital technologies to combat the virus. This book focuses on the crises and impact of COVID-19 pandemic in our society. The marginalised group of our society has very badly affected by this world pandemic those are connected to Indian grassroots' economy. Agriculture is the important and major source of livelihood and employment for the Indian society. On the other hand agriculture-related services, schemes, beneficiaries, are the major sources of livelihood of the people. During the last two years Indian agricultural sectors has badly destroy by the corona pandemic.

The coronavirus is forever changing the way we live and work. Some of the behaviours that emerged during the crisis, such as widespread digital adoption, will outlast the pandemic, long after restrictions on activity are lifted. Organizations must respond to these behavioural changes and meet emerging customer demands in order to remain competitive.

This Volume is possible with the blessing of our parents and family members whose continues inspiration guided us for publications this book in time. Our sincere thanks to all the chapter contributors without their contributions this edited volume would not have been possible. As a whole the book got the complete shape because of the great initiative of Notion press. Finally, we do hereby declare that the chapter contributed by the contributors are of their own views; if any discrepancies or legal issues arise out of this publication the contributors will be responsible for this; the editors or publishers will not bear the responsibility.

Mr.KrittibasDatta
Dr.MuktaGoyal

CHAPTER ONE

An Analysis on How Covid-19 Puts Women At More Risk Than Men In India

Dr.Mukta Goyal

Introduction

The COVID-19 pandemic has been a major shock to our societies and economies, highlighting society's reliance on women on the front lines and at home, while also exposing structural inequalities in every sphere, from health to the economy, security to social protection. Women and girls face disproportionate impacts with far-reaching consequences in times of crisis, when resources are strained and institutional capacity is limited, which are amplified in contexts of fragility, conflict, and emergencies. Hard-won victories for women's rights are also in jeopardy. Responding to the pandemic is about more than just redressing long-standing inequalities; it's also about creating a resilient world that benefits everyone, with women at the forefront of recovery.

"It is the responsibility of women to hold the social fabric together – whether at home, in health centres and schools, or caring for the elderly – all of this is unpaid care work (and it continues to increase)," explains Mita Lonkar of the Chaitanya Foundation in New Delhi, India, one of many UN Women NGO partners in India providing critical support to women and their families as the country struggles to cope with the COVID-19 pandemic's second wave.

"Because the majority of those on the front lines of the pandemic are women, resources such as healthcare, education, and training for women are critical," Lonkar adds. "Women are especially vulnerable economically because their personal finances are weaker and their employment opportunities are limited."

Since January 2020, India has reported over 27 million cases of COVID-19 infection and over 300,000 deaths – figures that many experts believe are significantly underestimated. Hospitals are running out of beds and oxygen, medications are running out, and vaccines are in short supply as infection rates rise. Cyclone Yaas made landfall last week, causing massive flooding and displacement in the country's coastal areas.

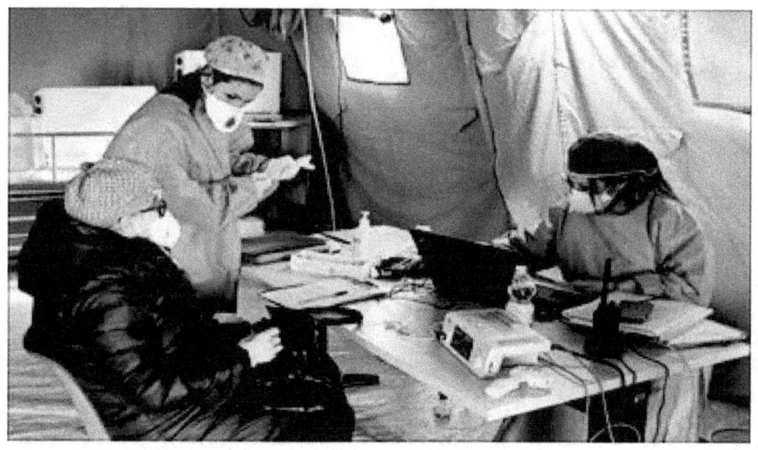

Source: thelancet.com

The emergency's scope is unprecedented, and as with any crisis, women and girls, particularly those from poor and marginalised communities, are among the worst affected. Women account for 34–42 percent of COVID-19 infections, according to data from at least seven states. The needs are vast, ranging from basic necessities such as food, personal protective equipment, hygiene and sanitation products, and vaccines to longer-term assistance to help women return to work and obtain start-up financing.

In India, the second wave of COVID-19 resulted in unprecedented losses. Without the means to absorb economic shocks and mitigate the health crisis, the poorest and most marginalised, including women and girls, face greater risks. They are providing for their families, maintaining their livelihoods, and leading efforts to combat climate.

UN Women and health sector experts respond to some frequently asked questions about COVID-19 and how it affects Indian women and girls.

The pandemic serves as a stark reminder of how important women are at all levels. Women are on the front lines of the COVID-19 response as health professionals, community volunteers, transportation and logistics managers, scientists, doctors, vaccine developers, and more. Women make up 70% of the health workforce worldwide, especially as nurses, midwives, and community health workers, and they also make up the majority of service staff in hospitals as cleaners, launderers, and caterers. Despite these figures, women are frequently left out of national and global decision-making on COVID-19. Furthermore, women are still paid significantly less than men.

Are women and girls at more risk of contracting COVID-19 than men?

The coronavirus has infected over 30 million people in India. COVID-19 is a virus that can infect people of all sexes and ages. Some women and girls, on the other hand, maybe at greater risk because they are poorer and lack information and resources, or because they work in the health and service sectors as caregivers and workers.

In India, women account for a large percentage of all healthcare workers, including more than 80% of nurses and midwives. However, they are largely absent from decision-making roles in the health sector, and they are paid significantly less than their male counterparts. Women make up only 13% of the COVID-19 task force at the national level.

Restrictive social norms, gender stereotypes, home quarantining, and resource diversion to combat the COVID-19 pandemic can limit women's access to health care and make them more vulnerable to health risks. Several women have been trapped at home with their perpetrators as a result of global lockdowns, and incidents and reports of violence against women have been on the rise around the world. Due to the COVID-19 emergency response and global lockdowns, women's access to sexual and reproductive health services has been severely hampered. Their mental health has been severely strained as a result of their multiple responsibilities.

Source: the leaflet.in

How has COVID-19 impacted women's employment in India?
Women made up only 24% of the workforce in India before the pandemic, but they accounted for 28% of all job losses as the pandemic spread. During the lockdown, women lost nearly two-thirds of their income, and as their unpaid workload increased, they were far more likely than men to report a lack of sleep. The increased household burden could make it more difficult for women to re-enter the workforce, resulting in long-term economic consequences. The crisis has disproportionately affected historically vulnerable women, such as Muslim, migrant, and single, separated, widowed, or divorced women.

Supporting women's recovery from the pandemic would be a wise investment for governments and could help mitigate the pandemic's long-term impact on future generations, according to a Dalberg study.

Source: iwwage.org

Women have been pushed out of work and into poverty as a result of wage disparities and the burden of unpaid care. Even before the pandemic, women's earned income in India was only one-fifth that of men's. During COVID-19, more women have lost jobs around the world, including in India. According to a recent report by the Center for Sustainable Employment at Azim Premji University in India, only 7% of men lost their jobs during the first lockdown in 2020, compared to 47% of women who lost their jobs and did not return to work by the end of the year. Women fared even worse in the informal sector. Between March and April of this year, 80 percent of rural Indian women working in informal jobs were employed.

Despite the hardships encountered during the research, interviews revealed many inspiring stories of women's resilience: women supporting entire villages as they navigated the health crisis, spreading awareness, and serving as community lifelines and frontline workers throughout the crisis. Many people made difficult decisions to keep their families afloat, such as providing family meals with fewer supplies and, in some cases, going without food to ensure that their children were fed. Some people took money out of their savings to pay for things like household supplies, food, and medicine, as well as internet packages for their children's continued education, for which many people also had to provide tutoring.

Women and children from the community gathered in Batla House, Okhla, New Delhi, at a Saheli Samanvay Kendra (SSK) community centre. The Indian government has established SSK community centres across the country to serve as local incubation centres for women's self-help groups, skill training, and public health information. The SSKs work in "Anganwadi" centres, which are part of the Indian public health care system and provide basic health care to rural and marginalised populations. These centres have remained open throughout the COVID-19 pandemic, providing free meals, immunizations, and health screenings for children, pregnant and lactating mothers, and assisting women in accessing government assistance programmes. Women learn tailoring and sewing, as well as computer skills and beautician techniques, at the SSK centre in Batla House.

Socio-Economic Impact of COVID-19 on Women Migrant Workers

In India, the COVID-19 pandemic has wreaked havoc on domestic migrant workers. This brief presents the key findings from a survey of 10,161 women migrant workers from 12 Indian states to address the pandemic's gendered impact on migrant workers. Women migrant workers were found to be burdened with the dual burden of earning a living and providing unpaid care at home, according to the study. Furthermore, compared to pre-pandemic levels, their incomes dropped by more than half during the pandemic. In light of this, this brief discusses the importance of social protection measures for Indian women migrant workers in the areas of food security, cash assistance, government health insurance, and domestic violence protection.

Has COVID-19 increased violence against women in India?

Violence against women remains a major threat to global public health and women's health during emergencies, according to the WHO. Domestic violence cases have increased since the COVID-19 outbreak began, according to reports from China, the United Kingdom, the United States, and other countries. In India, the National Commission for Women has reported an increase in the number of reported cases of violence. Women's vulnerability to violence can be exacerbated by stress, disruption of social and protective networks, and a lack of access to services.

Source: theguardian.com

Gender-based violence is on the rise as a result of economic and social pressures, as well as movement restrictions and cramped living quarters. Prior to the pandemic, it was estimated that one in every three women would face violence at some point in their lives, a human rights violation with a USD 1.5 trillion economic costs. As overburdened healthcare systems and disrupted justice systems struggle to respond, many of these women are now trapped at home with their abusers and are at increased risk of other forms of violence. Online forms of violence against women and girls in chat rooms, gaming platforms, and other places are likely to increase as more people spend time online with movement restrictions in place. –– Women as they navigate deserted urban or rural public spaces and transportation services under lockdown, essential and informal workers –– such as doctors, nurses, and street vendors –– are at increased risk of violence. Economic effects of the pandemic are likely to increase sexual exploitation and child marriage, putting women and girls in fragile economies and refugee situations at risk. UN Secretary-General António Guterres called for an end to all forms of violence everywhere, from war zones to people's homes, in April, and for all efforts to be focused on ending the pandemic.

Domestic violence shelter and support services have been classified as "essential" by the Indian government, marking a significant step forward in the COVID-19 response. In India, 700 One-Stop-Crisis centres remained open during the first and second waves of the pandemic, assisting over 300,000 women who had been abused and required shelter, legal assistance, and medical attention.

Another positive step is the current draught of the anti-trafficking bill, which will be tabled in Parliament soon and will increase penalties for perpetrators and make reporting of such crimes mandatory.

Is the COVID-19 vaccine safe for pregnant or menstruating women?

While reports suggest that men, the elderly, and people with weakened immune systems are the most vulnerable to COVID-19, the greater caregiving role that women and girls are expected to fulfil may jeopardise their mental health and well-being.

COVID-19 vaccines have not been shown to cause harmful side effects in menstruating, pregnant, or lactating women. In addition, there is no evidence that COVID-19 vaccines cause infertility. In fact, if COVID-19 is contracted during pregnancy, there is a higher risk of severe symptoms.

The World Health Organization has also confirmed that women who are breastfeeding can safely receive the vaccine, and that no active COVID-19 disease-causing virus has been detected in breast milk. Vaccinating lactating mothers has been shown to be effective.

How can we support women and girls in India during the COVID-19 crisis?

Social workers use public awareness campaigns to ensure that women receive verified information about disease prevention and vaccination, as well as to raise public awareness about gender-based violence. Through our programmes, we are providing women with access to education and vocational training via digital and distance learning, as well as assisting them in finding employment and starting small businesses. In COVID-safe spaces, we collaborate with our national partners to provide survivors of gender-based violence with shelter, financial and legal assistance, and medical assistance.

Discussion and Recommendations

Every crisis impacts women and girls differently than men, because of existing gender norms and inequalities. To build back better and equal from the COVID-19 crisis, policy, investment and action must be shaped by women and girls and deliberately target them.

What can be done to mitigate the risk to family planning programs?

• Social marketing and FP service delivery organisations could help the government ensure a steady supply of reversible contraception and relieve some of the strain on the public health system.

• Self-care items such as condoms, oral contraceptive pills, emergency contraceptive pills, pregnancy test kits, and sanitary pads should be readily available in pharmacies. Furthermore, ensuring the continuity of the contraceptive supply chain is critical in order to avoid stockouts in districts and PHCs.

• To ensure continued access to family planning services, ASHAs and other community-based health workers should be supported.

• Family planning counseling should be available through helplines, telemedicine services, community radios, chatbots, and mobile services.

• In this time of crisis, the government should make use of partnerships with NGOs to support information and service delivery. In this time of crisis, the government has recognised the critical role of NGOs in providing services to vulnerable groups. Many women and children will need to be able to access essential non-COVID-19 healthcare services, so ensuring easy mobility and smooth operations of NGOs providing health and family planning services will be critical.

Source: feminisminindia.com

What can be done to address mental health issues stemming from the COVID-19 pandemic?

• Women's psychological support services should be integrated into primary health care.

• The creation of a comprehensive crisis prevention and intervention system that includes epidemiological monitoring, screening, referral, and targeted intervention to alleviate psychological distress.

• Public awareness campaigns to ensure that vulnerable groups, such as women, are well informed about mental health services' availability and accessibility.

• Increased research funding for mental health.

• Strengthening mental health services by establishing a cadre of trained professionals.

What can be done to address violence against women during the COVID-19 response?

• Governments and policymakers should include measures to address violence against women in COVID-19 preparedness and response plans.

• A public health response to violence against women is being developed.

• Providing survivors of violence and early detection cases with preventive, curative, and systematic referral support.

• Educating healthcare providers so that they can provide better care and counselling to victims of violence.

• Hotlines, telemedicine services, shelters, rape crisis centres, and counselling for victims of violence must all be made available.

• Greater emphasis on violence reporting in COVID-19 response plans.

Conclusion

As the worst of the pandemic fades and vaccination rates steadily rise, rebuilding India's economy and bringing the newly impoverished back into the middle class is a critical policy challenge made more complicated by the country's uniquely gendered nature and the fact that, as in most crises, women bear the brunt and have the most difficult time recovering.

Recognizing women's physical ordeals is, without a doubt, the first step toward empowering them. Too many of them are anecdotal due to a lack of academic or policy intervention to assess their statistical significance. It is also critical that the government enlists the help of existing organised corporate structures to implement compassionate labour policies, particularly from a political standpoint. a gendered perspective While recognising invisible household chores has its own set of challenges, and it's difficult to catalyse interventions in the domestic sphere, the structured and easily amendable work sectors must help India's women reclaim their lost morale. Existing skill-building programmes run by the government of India, such as the Pradhan Mantri Kaushal Vikas Yojana scheme (PMKVY), must be implemented uniformly across our urban spheres, identifying capable and determined women and cultivating in them the entrepreneurial appetite to create jobs and responsibilities as the economy recovers.

Finally, the transformation must come from within us. As women move outdoors, work must be shared responsibly by all. Stakeholders must band together to prioritise women's education and health, as well as to actualize women's empowerment through education and health.

References

- Dada, S., Ashworth, H. C., Bewa, M. J., & Dhatt, R. (2021). Words matter: political and gender analysis of speeches made by heads of government during the COVID-19 pandemic. BMJ global health, 6(1), e003910.
- Gausman, J., & Langer, A. (2020). Sex and gender disparities in the COVID-19 pandemic. Journal of Women's Health, 29(4), 465-466.
- Madgavkar, A., White, O., Krishnan, M., Mahajan, D., & Azcue, X. (2020). COVID-19 and gender equality: Countering the regressive effects. McKinsey Global Institute.
- Chatterjee, S. S., Chakrabarty, M., Banerjee, D., Grover, S., Chatterjee, S. S., & Dan, U. (2021). Stress, sleep and psychological impact in healthcare workers during the early phase of COVID-19 in India: a factor analysis. Frontiers in Psychology, 12, 473.
- https://www.google.com/ search?q=how+covid+19+impacts+women+and+girls+in+India.&oq=
- how+covid+19+impacts+women+and+girls+in+India.&aqs
- =chrome..69i57.10420j0j4&sourceid=chrome&ie=UTF-8
- https://dalberg.com/our-ideas/the-disproportionate-impact-of-covid-19-on-women-in-india/
- https://www.unwomen.org/en/news/stories/2021/7/faq-women-and-covid-19-in-india?gclid=CjwKCAiA_omPBhBBEiwAcg7smR6MQtVsUnqm
- JDFLtXgoZBvSkiY7dJaq_ehhkDaITKpymf000DKd0hoC81QQAvD_BwE

- https://www.outlookindia.com/website/story/opinion-an-indefinite-pandemic-tracing-the-covid-impact-on-indias-female-workforce/393124
- https://asia.nikkei.com/Opinion/COVID-19-s-devastating-impact-on-Indian-women

CHAPTER TWO

Impact of Corona Pandemic on Agricultural Economy in Chhattisgarh

*Chiranjibi Sabar**Dinesh Kumar Dahariya*

Abstract

Agriculture is an important and major source of livelihood and employment for Indian society. Indian agriculture accounts for 17-18 percent of India's gross domestic product (GDP) and it provides 50% employment to the whole of our country. It can be easily said that agriculture is the backbone of our Indian economy (Economic Survey, 2017–2018). Indian agriculture helps to satisfy and fulfill people's basic needs such as food, shelter, and clothing. Indian agriculture is largely dependent on the monsoon season. In our country, only half of the cropped area is covered by irrigation systems. The Indian rural economy is primarily dependent on agriculture and also the rural farmers are largely dependent on monsoon rains.

Agriculture and agriculture-related services, schemes, beneficiaries, are the major sources of livelihood of the people. Around 70 percent of Indian farmers depend on agriculture in rural areas. Agriculture plays an important role in the economic development of our country. Almost all the activities revolve around agriculture. It employs around 60 percent of the total workforce in the country who still depend on farming activities for their livelihood security (Swaminathan, 2009).

Livelihood is a set of economic activities, involving self-employment and or wage employment by making use of one's endowments, which can be human and material. The use of human and material resources is primarily made use of to generate adequate resources, which can be either cash or non-cash. These resources are made use of by the rural individuals to sustain their livelihoods in an enhanced manner.

Key words- agriculture, Livelihood, economy, and challenges.

Introduction

Agricultural economics is a branch of economics that is concerned with problems relating to agriculture. Agriculture economics is an economy that deals with the production, consumption, exchange, and distribution of agricultural food grains in the market in which people satisfy their wants or needs. The wants or needs of the farmers are based on their demands of agriculture inputs in the village market. The word agriculture economy consists of two words i.e., Agriculture and Economics.

The word, agriculture is derived from the two Latin words ager, which refers to the soil, and cultura, which refers to its cultivation. Agriculture can be defined as the cultivation of crops, traditional patterns of cropping systems, traditional use of fertilizer, pesticides, their harvesting, storage, packaging, and production of crop plants or other agricultural inputs products. The word 'Economics' is derived from the two Greek words 'Oikos', which means 'Households', and 'Nomos', which means 'Management'. So, economics means household management.

Adam Smith, a classical economist defined economics as "An inquiry into the nature and causes of the wealth of nations" in his book, entitled "Wealth of Nations". He is regarded as the 'Father of Economics (Smith, 1776). Alfred Marshall, in his book "Principles of Economics" defined "Political Economy or Economics as a study of mankind in the ordinary business of life, it examines that part of individual and social action which is most closely connected with the attainment and with the use of the material requisites of well- being (Marshall, 1890).

Agricultural economics as a specialized form of pure science of economics and emphasizes the role which plays in coordinating general economics and the natural sciences. More specifically, agricultural economics includes farm management, land economics, prices and statistics, agricultural policy, production economics, marketing, agricultural law, and farm credit (Black, 1953).

Brief about the state

As per population census 2011, the total population of Chhattisgarh state is 2,55,45,198. Whereas, male population is 1,28,32,895 and the female population is 1,27,12,303. Of which male and female comprise 50.23% and 49.76% respectively. The scheduled caste and scheduled tribes' population of the state comprises 12% and 32% respectively (Sharma et al., 2014).

The study was conducted at Mungeli, which is a newly formed recently and it became a district on 1 January 2012 by Chief Minister Dr. Raman Singh inaugurated the new district. The district comprises three Tehsil namely, Mungeli, Patharia, and Lormi. It is situated in the north-northwestern part of Chhattisgarh state and it is surrounded by Kawardha district in the west, Bemetara district in the south, and Bilaspur district in the east. Mungeli district is situated on the bank of the rain-fed Agar River, which originates from Teliapani, Kabirdham district at an elevation of 735m, the high hills of the Maikal Range of Central India (Bhardwaj, 2019).

Climate and irrigation facilities

The climate of the district is ideal with a beautiful monsoon, a mild summer, and a bearable winter. The average rainfall of the district is (June to October),1071 mm per annum. In the Mungeli district, 47.30% of the area comes under irrigated conditions during rabi season. Total 60257.00 Hectares, is irrigated and 75423.00 Hectares, is unirrigated (Bhardwaj, 2019).

Patterns of cultivation

Chhattisgarh is known for rice cultivation and is called the 'rice bowl 'of India. Paddy, maize, jowar, groundnut, gram, and wheat are major crops grown in Chhattisgarh. About 80% of the population of the state is rural and the main livelihood of the villagers is agriculture and agriculture-based small industry (Sharma et al., 2014). The district has one of the most important potential area in terms of production, and productivity of different crops. This district comes under the plain region of Chhattisgarh state.

Map No. 01. Map of the District

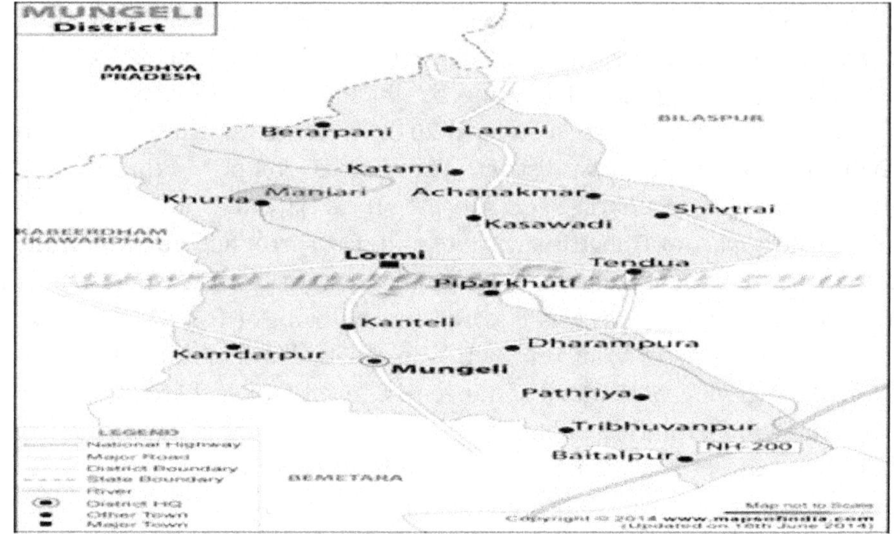

(Source- Google Map, 2021)

Nawagaon Dayali

The present study was carried out at Nawagaon Dayali village of Lormi block in Mungeli district, Chhattisgarh. It is situated 20 km away from sub-district headquarter Lormi and 85km away from district headquarter Bilaspur (now in Mungeli). Nawagaon Dayali village is a Gram Panchayat.

Chart No. 01. Village population

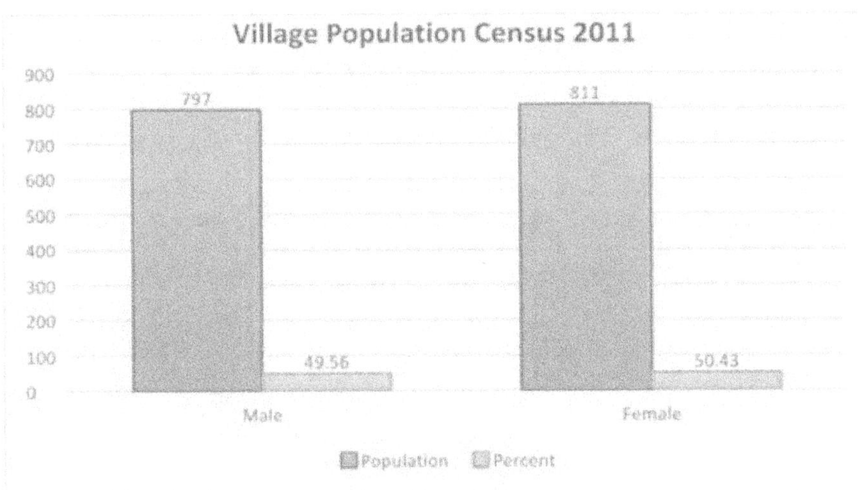

(Source- Census, 2011)

The above chart shown the total population of the village has 397 households and the total population of Nawagaon Dayali village comprises 1,608 off them, male population consists 797 (49.56%) and female consists 811 (60.43%).

Chart No. 02. Occupational status

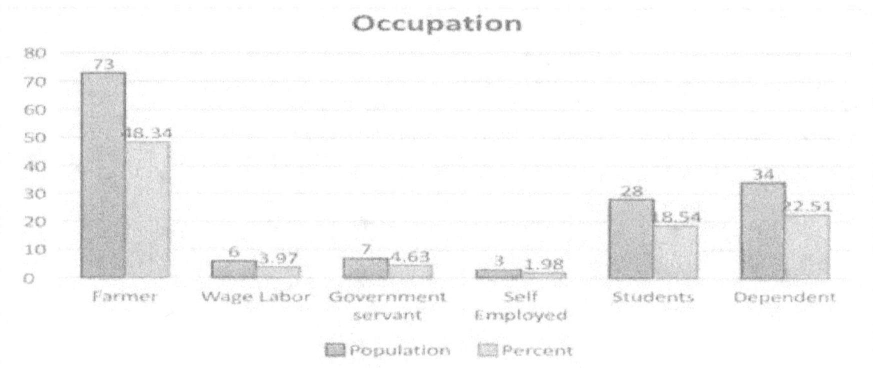

(Source- Primary data, June 2021)

The above chart depicts the occupation of family members. The study shows that the primary occupation of study village persons includes around 48.34% have adhered to Farmer/agriculture, 3.97% are wage labor, 4.63% are government servant, 1.98% are self-employed, 18.54% belongs to the students, and 22.51 are dependent on his parents.

Chart No. 03. Status of ration cards

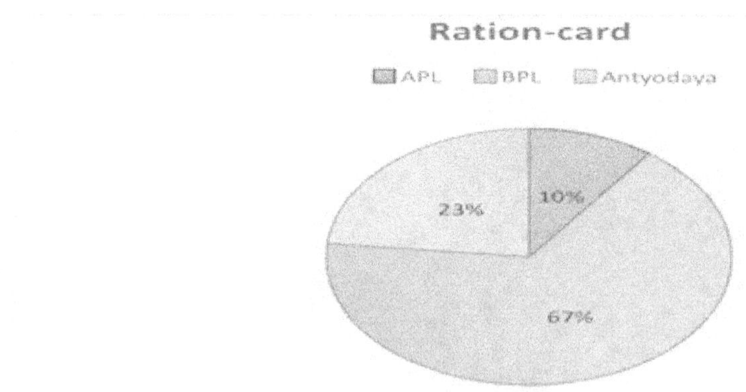

(Source- Primary data, June 2021)

The above chart depicts the status of ration card availability in the study households. Out of 30 households, the distribution of APL is found 10%, BPL is found in 66.66% and antyodya is found as 23.33% of the study households in the study village.

Table No. 1. Annual income status of the village

Table No. 1. Annual income status of the village

Annual HHS Income	Population	Percentage
20,000- 30,000	3	10
31,000- 38,000	9	30
39,000- 45,000	7	23.33
46,000-50, 000	6	20
> 50,000	5	16.66
Total	30	100

(Source- Primary data, June 2021)

The above table shown that the annual income of households in the studied village. Where 30% households' income is 31,000-38,000, 23.33% households' income is 39,000-45, 000, 20% households' income is 46,000-50, 000, 16.66% households' income is above 50,000 and 10% households' income is 20,000-30, 000.

The village has paddy as the major crop produced by the villagers. Very few villagers cultivate the vegetables in their homestead land for their consumption. In this village, there is no shortage of water both in the rainy and summer season and does not affect the agriculture in the village. Because in this village, the source of water is the Rajiv Gandhi Dam (also known as Khudiya Dam) near to the village within 5Km. This dam electrifies and supplies the water body by canal to the villager's farmland and this dam is the only major source of water in this village, the farmers irrigated his farmland by the use of this water body source. In this village, the villagers entirely depended on Rajiv Gandhi Dam, if there was a shortage of water in the rainy season. Most of the villagers have their sanitation unit within their households. However, very few villagers go outside for open defecation.

Crops cultivation of the village

The Nawagaon Dayali village is majorly dependent upon monsoon agriculture. The major cultivated crops are paddy, tivara, and tur (arhar) (Table 4.1). The majority of the village population grew the Paddy as their first crop. Paddy is the staple crop of the village and they constitute the staple diet of the farmers and agricultural Labour. There is no impact on the Paddy farming of the farmers. The study found that most of the farmers of the village said that their annual production of the Paddy has increased in the Kharif year 2020-21 rather than the year 2019-20

Table No. 02. Distribution of different types of crops cultivation

Table No. 02. Distribution of different types of crops cultivation

Categories	Crops Name	Number of Farmers	Percent
First crop	Paddy/ Rice	14	46.66
Second crop	Tivra	12	40
Third crop	Pigeon Pea	4	13.33
Total		30	100

(Source- Primary data, June 2021)

The above table shows the preference of the crops to be grown by the farmers in the study village. We can see that the majority 46.66% farmers preferred the paddy, which is the first crop grown by the farmers and 40% of the farmers preferred the Tivra, which is the second crop grown by the farmers and only 13.33% of the farmers preferred that Pigeon Pea, is the third pulses grown by farmers.

Impact on seed availability

The availability of seeds for crop production in the study village seeding availability was almost unaffected between now and the summer season during the lockdown. Most of the village farmers in Nawagaon Dayali village are to hold previous seasons of the paddy seeds and use these seasons. Some village farmers buy the paddy seed on government and private mandi stock at the rate of Rs 730 per bag or bori (30kg) and grow it on the farmland. So there are no problems or impacts faced by the village farmers on the seed availability during the lockdown.

Chart No. 04. Types of seeds used by the farmers

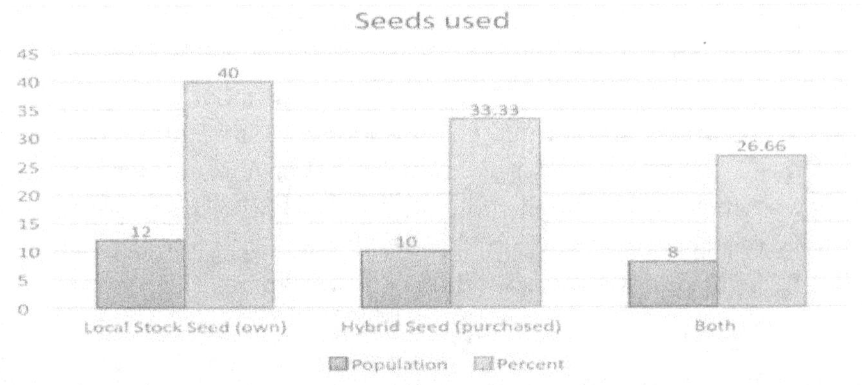

(Source- Primary data, June 2021)

The above chart shows the purposes or types of paddy seed used by the farmers for cultivation. The highest proportion of the population 12 households (40%) uses local stock seeds of paddy, 10 households (33.33%) purchase hybrid paddy seed from the mandi, while 8 households (26.66%) used both types of paddy seed for growing in the farmland

Shortage of fertilizers

Due to the disturbance of global trade, farmers faced a huge shortage of agricultural inputs like fertilizer and pesticides. During the lockdown, there is little shortage of fertilizer to be found in the study village of Nawagaon Dayali. The farmers are to hold their unsold previous seasons of produce for a longer period of time. This has led to a reduction in food quality as well as an increase in the cost of production. Due to the spread of the pandemic and the lockdown that had a significant impact on the farm input prices of commodities in agriculture fertilizer like urea, DAP, Potash, NPK etc. The study found that the village farmers buy the DAP fertilizer at the rate of Rs 1200 (50kg Bag), Urea Rs 266 (45kg Bag), NPK Rs 1185 (50kg Bag) and

Potash Rs 1000 per bag from the government purchase center in the Kharif year 2020-21 during the lockdown.

Labour unavailability:

The study found that the non-availability of labor has hurt and impacted only those village farmers in the study village which has a large acre of farmland. The small farmers do not need much manual labor for harvesting and storage of paddy seeds. The shortage of migrant labour has resulted in a sharp increase in daily wages for harvesting crops. Paddy and Tivara often do not have to depend on large numbers of manual labour and agricultural labor was disturbed at work due to transportation problems. Labor work under the MGNREGA (Mahatma Gandhi National Rural Employment Guarantee Schemes) has stopped due to the lockdown. This decreases the income of the labor households.

Chart No. 05.Shortage of labor during lockdown

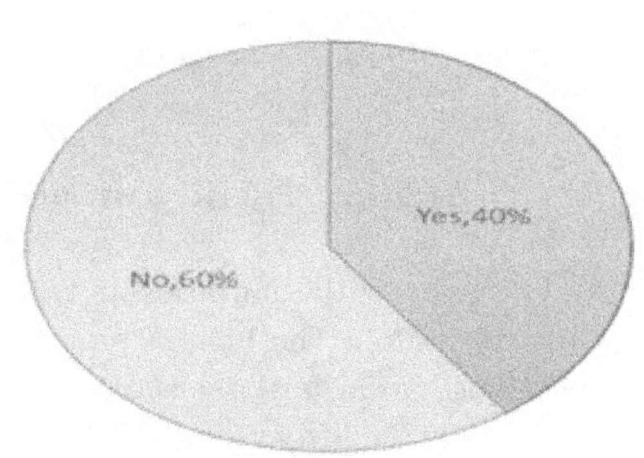

(Source- Primary data, June 2021)

The above chart shows the problem of the non-availability of workers being faced by the farmers during the lockdown. We can see that 60% of the farmers did not face problems related to unavailability or shortage of labor, whereas only 40% of farmers faced problems related to unavailability or shortage of labor during the lockdown.

Impact on transportation:

The study found that some farmers faced difficulties in transportation of crop sales during the lockdown. Because the government has a ban on the movement of the vehicle. Farmers face difficulties because of the guidelines of the government for selling their grains at the local market and also the Government Mandis. and Due to the lockdown, the cost of vehicles and labor price increases. The small farmers have faced problems to afford the vehicle price. Some farmers have their own vehicles, they do not face problems related to the transportation of grains at the grain purchase center. The study also found the high cost of labor price and it creates problems with their transportation of grains. The farmers of the studied village faced difficulties due to lack of transportation facilities, poor road infrastructure, shutting down of rural markets and shops and mandis.

Chart No. 06. Transportation problem faced by the farmers

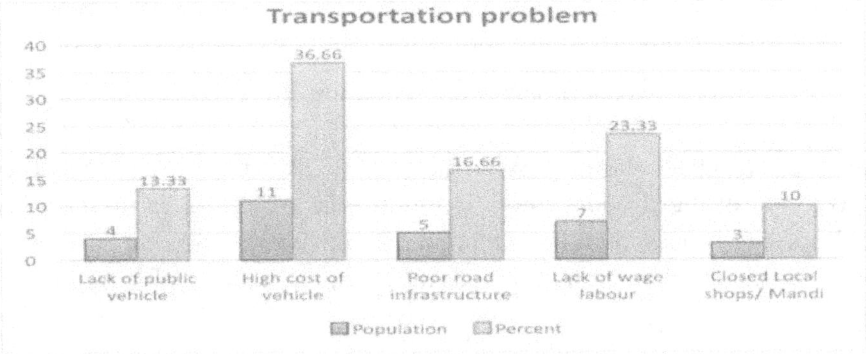

(Source- Primary data, June 2021)

The above chart shows that the respondents faced difficulties in transportation of crop sales during the lockdown. Majorly about 36.66% of farmers were facing problems due to vehicle transactions, 23.33% of farmers are facing problems by non-availability or lack of labor, 16.66% of farmers are facing problems of poor road infrastructure, 13.33% of farmers are facing problems of lack of public vehicle, and 10% farmers are facing problem by the market closed during the lockdown.

Chart No. 07. Type of storage problem:

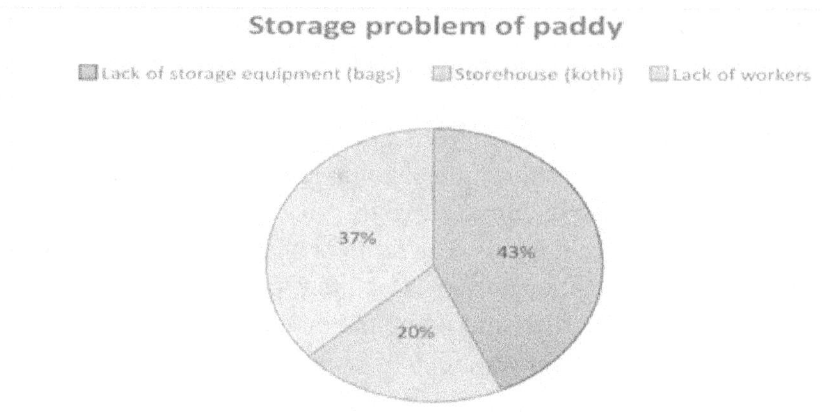

(Source- Primary data, June 2021)

The above chart shows how farmers faced difficulties in storing the paddy crop during the lockdown. It found that 43.33% of farmers faced problems due to lack of storage equipment like bags, sacks, etc., 36.66 % due to shortage of labor, and 20% because of unavailability of storehouses (Kothi).

The farmers faced difficulties in storing the grains. Most of them faced due to the lack of storage equipment bags, shortage of labor for storage, and lack of warehouse (Kothi) in their homes. The Government Mandis did not provide an accurate package of bags to the farmers. The farmers stored their Paddy grains in the old sack (Bora) and small bori. The study showed that very few farmers have warehouse Kothi, the storage facility of the grains in their homes.

Problems of price reduction

The study found that the prices of agricultural products have decreased during the lockdown because of lack of market access and stoppage of transportation. The costs of labour have increased and farmers are facing huge losses. The study showed that the farmers are not satisfied with the price which is fixed by the central Government for Mandis, the price is very low as farmers say. The farmers do not get the right price of their agri-products, the Central Government announced the minimum support price (MSP) for paddy Rs 2500 per quintal at Government Mandis, but the Central Government could not fulfill the promise. The farmers did not get the fixed amount according to their production and due to this, the farmers feel that there was no profit. During the lockdown, in the Kharif year 2020-21, the central government had fixed the purchase price of normal paddy at Rs 1,868 and that of Grade-A paddy at Rs 1,888 per quintal. Farmers were not satisfied with the price of paddy grains. In the Kharif year 2019-20, farmers could get a profit of only Rs 1815 per quintal for normal paddy and Rs 1835 per quintal for grade-A paddy.

Impact on harvesting

The study found that plowing, plowing the seed, spraying herbicide, insecticide and fertilizer are the works of men while weeding, and caring for livestock are the activities of women. However, there are somewhere the division is less clear, such as harvesting, land clearing, and planting which are shared by both men and women in the household. The study found that the working of labor to the farmers' farmland provides at the Rs 100 per labor including of both men and women. Family households' children and 18 years above individuals are also helped to involve in the work of harvesting and storage of grains.

Conclusion

The present study explored many problems, how the corona pandemic impacted the agricultural sector during the lockdown. The study found out that, the majority of the villagers grow three main crops viz., paddy crops and tivara and pulses. Paddy or rice is the staple crop or food of Nawagaon Dayali villagers. Paddy is their life-long traditional cropping pattern around the whole community of the village. Very few households grow vegetables and there were no major impacts found in their traditional agricultural system. The study found a minor impact on the agriculture economy. There are some large landlord and land hold farmers who faced problems like unavailability of labor, and unavailability of labor was seen much in the large farmers, who have large numbers of farmlands. The unavailability of workers was not much impacted in small farmers, who have very few farmlands. The small agriculture farmers mostly contribute the source of income in the work of outsider areas. The small migrant laborers of the village who still depend on the work of the outsider were mostly affected, when the lockdown was announced and extended day today and they returned to their native village and entirely dependent on the work of farms but there were unnecessary increases of labor. The study reveals that most farmers of the village face problems with the sale of their grains due to the closure of transportation facilities and poor road infrastructure.

Most of the farmers faced problems due to lack of storage facilities, the government mandis were not properly provided the bags and bori to the farmers for storing the grains. Most of the farmers have faced problems with token facilities due to lockdown. They were standing in long lines in the token distribution centers and the government has not taken special and easier measures for these problems. The token has not been provided in one day, farmers have rounded the token distribution center day today. The study found that there was no impact of agricultural production, the production of the grains but the farmers were not satisfied with the rate fixed by the government for selling in mandi, the price fell at very low. Farmers did not get accurate prices according to their crop production. The central government has already announced the minimum support price (MSP) of paddy grains at the government mandis at Rs 2500 per quintal for the Kharif year 2020-21, but due to the extension of lockdown, the central government has not cooperated in fulfilling at the promised price and not provided the fixed rate of paddy grains to the farmers. During the lockdown period, in Kharif years 2020-21, out of 2500 per quintal of paddy grains, farmers benefited only for their paddy grains in government mandis at Rs. 1868 per quintal for common paddy grains, while grade A paddy grains were purchased at Rs 1,888 per quintal in the year 2020-21. The farmers of the study village are not satisfied with this decreasing price of paddy grains provided by the central government, the price was very low as some farmers said. While, during the Kharif year 2019-20, the central government had fixed the MSP of paddy grains at Rs 1815 per quintal for common or normal paddy grains, while Rs 1835 per quintal grade A paddy grains and farmers got only this accurate price, decided by the central government in the year 2019-20.

References

- Bhardwaj, C. S. (2019a). District survey report Mungeli. Directorate of Geology and Mining Chhattisgarh. Published.
- Bhardwaj, C. S. (2019b). District survey report Mungeli. Directorate of Geology and Mining Chhattisgarh. Published.
- Black, J. D. (1953). Introduction to economics for agriculture. Macmillan Company.
- Economic Survey. (2017–2018). Role of agriculture in Indian economy. ForumIAS Offline Guidance Centre.

- Marshall, A. (1890). Principles of Economics (Vol. 1). London: Macmillan and Co. and New York.
- Sharma, H. O., Rathi, D., Chouhan, R. S., & Niranjan, H. K. (2014a). State of agriculture in Chhattisgarh (No. 113). Jawaharlal Nehru Krishi Vishwa Vidyalaya, Jabalpur (M.P.).
- Sharma, H. O., Rathi, D., Chouhan, R. S., & Niranjan, H. K. (2014b). State of agriculture in Chhattisgarh (No. 113). Jawaharlal Nehru Krishi Vishwa Vidyalaya, Jabalpur (M.P.).
- Smith, A. (1776). An inquiry into the nature and causes of the wealth of nations: Complete five unabridged books (Illustrated ed.). Chump Change.
- Swaminathan, M. S. (2009). Agriculture and food systems. Science and Sustainable Food Security, 331–343. https://doi.org/10.1142/9789814282116_0025

The Global Epidemic Of Covid – 19 And Its Impact On India

**Swarup Biswas*

Introduction

The global epidemic of Covid-19 refers to the worldwide outbreak and rapid spread of Coronavirus Disease 2019 (Covid-19). The disease is caused by a special virus called coronavirus 2 (SARS-Cavi-2 virus), which causes severe acute respiratory symptoms. The Chinese government imposed emergency blockades on Wuhan and other cities in Hubei Province, which surrounded Uhan, but failed to stop the spread of the disease, which quickly spread to other parts of China and later to the rest of the world. The World Health Organization recognized the disease as a global pandemic on March 11, 2020. Multiple strains of the SARS-Cavi-2 virus have emerged and are prevalent in many countries around the world; Of these, alpha, beta and delta species are the most prevalent. As of October 26, 2021, more than 244.7 million people worldwide have been infected with the coronavirus disease, and about 49 million of them have died, making it one of the deadliest global epidemics in human history.

The symptoms of Coronavirus Disease 2019 vary from person to person. Some people do not experience any symptoms at all, while for some other people they are severe. Older patients and those who suffer from one or more other long-term illnesses, regardless of age, are more likely to have a severe form of the disease. When a person infected with coronavirus 2019 coughs or sneezes, millions of tiny mucus particles thrown into the air begin to float in the air, and the virus can be transmitted to his or her body if another nearby person inhales the infected air. Even very small amounts of virus particles can float in the air due to normal breathing. The virus can also be present on the surface material for hours or days by sneezing or coughing on a particle table or any other surface or by touching with the infected hand. It can enter the body, but transmission is rare. The virus is more likely to spread to nearby people, but there is a risk of spreading the virus farther than usual inside buildings or rooms and in areas with poor ventilation.

Once infected, the virus is likely to be transmitted from one person to another in about 20 days. The patient is most contagious when he or she begins to show symptoms, but it is possible for the disease to be transmitted before the onset of symptoms. However, in most cases, it can take two to 14 days or more. The most common symptoms of the disease are fever, cough, and shortness of breath. Acute respiratory symptoms can develop and, if taken in a more severe form, can lead to the death of the patient. Even after apparently recovering, some patients may have long-term circulatory health risks (heart disease, cerebral hemorrhage, etc.) after Covid-19.

As of October 2021, no antiviral drugs have been approved or approved by the authorities for the treatment of the disease. In the hospital, the treatment of the severe stage of the disease is mainly to relieve the symptoms and provide supportive treatment so that the patient can recover slowly on his own. In the second half of 2020, several vaccines were introduced in different countries and since December 2020, Covid-19 vaccination activities have been going on in different countries of the world. In addition to vaccinations, to prevent the spread of the disease, wear a medical mask or health mask covering the nose and mouth in public places, maintain social and physical distance with other people, use improved ventilation and ventilation systems inside buildings, adhere to etiquette when sneezing and coughing. Hand washing is recommended to disinfect, prevent surface infections, monitor patients, and self-isolate in potentially infected individuals. Quarantine, lockdown, curfew, postponement and cancellation of events and closure of various businesses and educational institutions, mandatory Covid-19 diagnostic test regulations, infectious person search, etc. Measures have also been taken at airports and railway stations to test for symptoms and the presence of the virus in the body, warning messages about traveling to heavily affected areas, etc. And universities have been declared closed nationally or locally, affecting the lives of about 1.2 billion students.

The global epidemic has disrupted socio-economic activities around the world. Many sports competitions and cultural events have been postponed or canceled. Misinformation and conspiracy theories about the virus have spread on the Internet, especially on social media. Also against people in China, East Asia, and Southeast Asia. Racism and xenophobia have increased. In the treatment of Covid-19 disease, there has been a conflict between developed and underdeveloped countries between inequality and restrictions on public health and personal freedoms.

Emergency measures and measures taken by the authorities to prevent the spread of coronavirus.

Since no vaccine for coronavirus disease 2019 is likely to be available before 2021, one of the keys to controlling the global epidemic is to reduce the peak of the epidemic (ie, the maximum number of infections per day), dubbed "epidemic curve leveling". Given; To this end, various measures are taken to reduce the rate of new infections. Reducing the rate of viral infections can reduce the risk of overexposure to the capacity of healthcare providers, ensure better health care for existing patients, reducing or prevent deaths due to lack of quality healthcare. In addition, the number of patients admitted can be controlled for a long time before the invention of vaccines or therapeutic drugs.

In addition to leveling the curve, another effort is required in parallel, which has been dubbed "straight line lifting". This means increasing the capacity of the healthcare system. This includes increasing the number of medical equipment and trained health workers, providing outpatient care, home care, and providing health education to the public.

Testing

According to the World Health Organization, the best way to prevent the spread of the coronavirus epidemic is to quickly identify infected people and isolate them from the community. For this reason, it is vital to carry out a comprehensive and intensive testing program as soon as possible. That's why businesses that manufacture test equipment need to multiply production to meet the acute shortage of such equipment in most of the world's countries. "We are sending a simple message to all countries – check, check, check," said Tedros Adhanom Gabrieusus, director-general of the World Health Organization. According to him, "all countries should be able to diagnose all suspected [coronavirus] infections. It is not possible to fight this disease blindly." It is not possible to isolate or isolate infected people without testing and thus breaking the chain of transmission. Testing, detection, and prevention have been successful in preventing the spread of the coronavirus epidemic in China, South Korea, and Singapore.

However, in many countries, it is limited to giving priority to testing only those who have returned, the elderly or the sick, and those who have mild symptoms or no symptoms are barred from participating in the tests. One reason for this is that most countries have not been able to test a large number of them. South Korea is an exception, as it has been carefully producing and storing test equipment for several years long before the current coronavirus epidemic (due to a previous outbreak of the Mars virus).

The impact of the coronavirus pandemic on India has been largely disruptive in terms of economic activity as well as a loss of human lives. Almost all the sectors have been adversely affected as domestic demand and exports sharply plummeted with some notable exceptions where high growth was observed. An attempt is made to analyze the impact and possible solutions for some key sectors.

Food & Agriculture

Since agriculture is the backbone of the country and a part of the government announced essential category, the impact is likely to be low on both primary agricultural production and usage of agro-inputs. Several state governments have already allowed free movement of fruits, vegetables, milk, etc. Online food grocery platforms are heavily impacted due to unclear restrictions on movements and stoppage of logistics vehicles. RBI and Finance Minister announced measures will help the industry and the employees in the short term. Insulating the rural food production areas in the coming weeks will hold a great answer to the macro impact of COVID-19 on the Indian food sector as well as the larger economy.

Aviation & Tourism

The contribution of the Aviation Sector and Tourism to our GDP stands at about 2.4% and 9.2% respectively. The Tourism sector served approximately 43 million people in FY 18-19. Aviation and Tourism were the first industries that were hit significantly by the pandemic. The common consensus seems to be that COVID will hit these industries harder than 9/11 and the Financial Crisis of 2008. These two industries have been dealing with severe cash flow issues since the start of the pandemic and are staring at a potential 38 million lay-offs, which translates to 70 percent of the total workforce. The impact is going to fall on both, White and Blue collar jobs. According to IATO estimates, these industries may incur losses of about

85 billion Rupees due to travel restrictions. The Pandemic has also brought about a wave of innovation in the fields of contactless boarding and travel technologies.

Telecom

There has been a significant amount of changes in the telecom sector of India even before the Covid-19 due to brief price wars between the service providers. Most essential services and sectors have continued to run during the pandemic thanks to the implementation of the 'work from home' due to restrictions. With over 1 billion connections as of 2019, the telecom sector contributes about 6.5 percent of GDP and employs almost 4 million people. Increased broadband usage had a direct impact and resulted in pressure on the network. Demand has been increased by about 10%. However, the Telco's are bracing for a sharp drop in adding new subscribers. As a policy recommendation, the government can aid the sector by relaxing the regulatory compliances and providing a moratorium for spectrum dues, which can be used for network expansions by the companies.

Pharmaceuticals

The pharmaceutical industry has been on the rise since the start of the Covid-19 pandemic, especially in India, the largest producer of generic drugs globally. With a market size of $55 billion during the beginning of 2020, it has been surging in India, exporting Hydroxychloroquine to the world, esp. to the US, UK, Canada, and the Middle East.

There has been a recent rise in the prices of raw materials imported from China due to the pandemic. Generic drugs are the most impacted due to heavy reliance on imports, disrupted supply-chain, and labour unavailability in the industry, caused by social distancing. Simultaneously, the pharmaceutical industry is struggling because of the government-imposed bans on the export of critical drugs, equipment, and PPE kits to ensure sufficient quantities for the country. The increasing demand for these drugs, coupled with hindered accessibility is making things harder. Easing the financial stress on the pharmaceutical companies, tax-relaxations, and addressing the labour force shortage could be the differentiating factors in such a desperate time.

Oil and Gas

The Indian Oil & Gas industry is quite significant in the global context – it is the third-largest energy consumer only behind USA and Chine and contributes to 5.2% of the global oil demand. The complete lockdown across the country slowed down the demand of transport fuels (accounting for

2/3rd demand in the oil & gas sector) as auto & industrial manufacturing declined and goods & passenger movement (both bulk & personal) fell. Though the crude prices dipped in this period, the government increased the excise and special excise duty to make up for the revenue loss, additionally, road cess was raised too. As a policy recommendation, the government may think of passing on the benefits of decreased crude prices to end consumers at retail outlets to stimulate demand.

Beyond Covid:

In view of the scale of disruption caused by the pandemic, it is evident that the current downturn is fundamentally different from recessions. The sudden shrinkage in demand & increased unemployment is going to alter the business landscape. Adopting new principles like 'shift towards localization, cash conservation, supply chain resilience, and innovation' will help businesses in treading a new path in this uncertain environment.

India's economy has shrunk to record levels in the current financial year – the country's government is deeply concerned after the release of this information.

In the three months since the lockdown on coronavirus in India, GDP has shrunk by about 24 percent, the highest in the country's history, according to official figures. This contraction has been seen in every aspect of the economy including manufacturing, construction, hotels, transportation, housing. April to June – The official three-month GDP shows that the economy has contracted in all areas except agriculture. The reason for the lockdown was that the country's economy had almost come to a standstill during the Covid epidemic – with the exception of food and drug production and power plants. That is why the growth rate in agriculture alone is 3.4%.

But is this record contraction of the economy just for the lockdown? Economist ProsenjitBasu said that even before the lockdown, India's economy was constantly shrinking and that the lockdown had only 'struck a blow'. "India's GDP growth has been steadily declining every quarter for the past two years. As investment has declined, so has exported. The main direction of the economy has been declining for a long time. But the so-called economy is twelve o'clock, "said Dr. ProsenjitBasu.The government itself has said that the calculation of 24% contraction is incomplete. Experts say this means that the contraction is likely to be even greater, as a full account of the unorganized sector may not be available.

A reflection of the stagnation of public life.

Billions of people are involved in the unorganized sector. Among them are migrant workers as well as bricklayers or city-village rickshaw pullers or small shopkeepers. Many of them had to go on hunger strike during the lockdown period unless students from different social organizations distributed food among them.

More than 12 crore people in India have lost their jobs due to coronavirus lockdown, according to a survey.

According to a study by the country's leading think tank, the Center for Monitoring the Indian Economy, 122 million people lost their jobs in India in the last month alone, most of them day laborers or small business workers. Economists also warn that the number of unemployed people will increase day by day – and not just in urban areas, but also in India's rural economy. When a sudden lockdown was imposed across India two months ago, the wheel of the economy virtually stopped at just four hours' notice.

Millions of workers in the real estate industry, street vendors, peddlers or rickshaw pullers – all had their bread and butter cut off overnight. According to a survey conducted by the Center for Monitoring Indian Economy (CMIE), a leading research institute in India, the number of people losing such jobs in the country at the end of April has reached around 12.5 crores.

Conclusion

In conclusion, in the absence of screening facilities for all people across the country, there is a serious risk of transmission of the asymptomatic virus to a large number of infected people even after public awareness, isolation, quarantine, and even blockade. Therefore, if comprehensive and rapid coronavirus testing is not available, even if the symptoms do not appear, keep everyone at home in a state of confinement and with limited mobility and social interaction. , House cleaning and disinfection, etc. methods must be followed very carefully.

Coronavirus Disease 2019 (Covid-19) or Coronavirus Infection Prevention: Coronavirus can spread from person to person in two main ways. The first process of infection occurs in two stages. Step 1: If a coronavirus-infected person coughs and sneezes out of the house without covering his face, the coronavirus may float in the air around him (within a radius of 1-2 meters) for several hours. Step 2: Coronavirus can enter the lungs of other people through the airways if they breathe in air containing particulate matter. The second process of coronavirus infection also occurs in a few steps. Step 1: If the coronavirus-infected person does not follow the coughing etiquette, the coronavirus will stick to his hands or objects.

Step 2: Now if the person touches the surface of any object with his coronavirus hand somewhere in his environment, then the coronavirus may stay on that surface for more than one day.

Step 3: Now if another person touches the coronavirus surface with his hand, the new person will get the coronavirus.

Step 4: Coronavirus cannot be transmitted to the body or lungs by hand, so now if a new person touches the nose, mouth or eyes with his newly-coronavirus hand, only then will the coronavirus enter the body through the exposed mucous membranes of those areas and enter the throat first. Later the lungs will begin to reproduce.

Therefore, if the coronavirus can be prevented at the beginning of the two coronavirus processes mentioned above and at each intermediate stage of transmission, then it is possible to successfully prevent the transmission of this virus and disease. The following tips on coronavirus prevention are a must-read.

Reference

- "COVID-19 Dashboard by the Center for Systems Science and Engineering (CSSE) at Johns Hopkins University (JHU)".ArcGIS। Johns Hopkins University.
- "Coronavirus disease (COVID-19) – World Health Organization".www.who.int২০২১-১০-২৩.
- "WHO Director-General's opening remarks at the media briefing on COVID-19 – 11 March 2020"।www.who.int "Getting your workplace ready for COVID-19" (PDF)। World Health Organization। "Questions and answers on COVID-19"। European Centre for Disease Prevention and Control.
- "Coronavirus disease (COVID-19)"।www.who.int.
- "Symptoms of Novel Coronavirus (2019-nCoV)"। US Centers for Disease Control and Prevention।১০ফেব্রুয়ারি২০২০।সংগ্রহেরতারিখ১১ফেব্রুয়ারি২০২০।
- "Coronavirus Disease 2019 (COVID-19)"। Centers for Disease Control and Prevention।১৬মার্চ২০২০।
- Rothan, Hussin A.; Byrareddy, Siddappa N. (২০২০-০৫-০১)। "The epidemiology and pathogenesis of coronavirus disease (COVID-19) outbreak"। Journal of Autoimmunity (ইংরেজিভাষায়)। 109: 102433।

- Bhattasali, Amitava(2 September 2020) India's economy has shrunk to record levels in the current financial year – the country's government is deeply concerned after the release of this information. BBC bangla.
- "Coronavirus Update: Masks And Temperature Checks In Hong Kong"। Nevada Public Radio (ইংরেজিভাষায়)। সংগ্রহের‍তারিখ ২০২১-১০-২৩।
- CDC (২০২০-০২-১১)। "COVID-19 and Your Health"। Centers for Disease Control and Prevention (ইংরেজিভাষায়)। সংগ্রহের‍তারিখ ২০২১-১০-২৩।
- Gilbertson, Jayme Deerwester and Dawn। "Coronavirus: US says 'do not travel' to Wuhan, China, as airlines issue waivers, add safeguards"। USA TODAY (ইংরেজিভাষায়)। ২০২০-০১-২৭ তারিখেমূলথেকেআ‍করাইভকরা। সংগ্রহের‍তারিখ ২০২১-১০-২৩।
- "In U.S. and Germany, Community Transmission Is Now Suspected"। The New York Times (ইংরেজিভাষায়)। ২০২০-০২-২৬। আইএসএসএন 0362-4331। সংগ্রহের‍তারিখ ২০২১-১০-২৩।

CHAPTER FOUR

Covid 19 Pandemic and Indian Tribes

**Krittibas Datta

Introduction

The coronavirus (COVID-19) pandemic poses a grave health threat to tribal peoples in India. Indigenous communities already experience poor access to healthcare, significantly higher rates of communicable and non-communicable diseases, lack of access to essential services, sanitation, and other key preventive measures, such as clean water, soap, disinfectant, etc. The Tribal peoples experience a high degree of socio-economic marginalization and are at disproportionate risk in public health emergencies, becoming even more vulnerable during this global pandemic, owing to factors such as their lack of access to effective monitoring and early-warning systems, and adequate health and social services.

As lockdowns continue in our countries from the last two year, with no timeline in sight, Tribal peoples who already face food insecurity, as a result of the loss of their traditional lands and territories, confront even graver challenges in access to food. With the loss of their traditional livelihoods, which are often land-based, many Indigenous peoples who work in traditional occupations and subsistence economies or in the informal sector will be adversely affected by the pandemic. The situation of indigenous women, who are often the main providers of food and nutrition to their families, is even graver.

India's Scheduled Tribe (ST) Population

As per 2011 census data India's Scheduled Tribe (ST) population, comprises 8.6% of the total population. The tribes have faced multiple vulnerabilities even before the pandemic. During the COVID-19 pandemic, these vulnerabilities were exacerbated and new challenges emerged for tribal populations. Most of these tribes are characterised by isolation, economic backwardness, poor infrastructure, and quality of healthcare. Poverty among Scheduled Tribe (ST) was 45.3% (rural) and 24.1% (urban) as compared to the national average of 25.7% in rural and 13.7% in urban areas in 2011–12 (MoTA 2018–19).

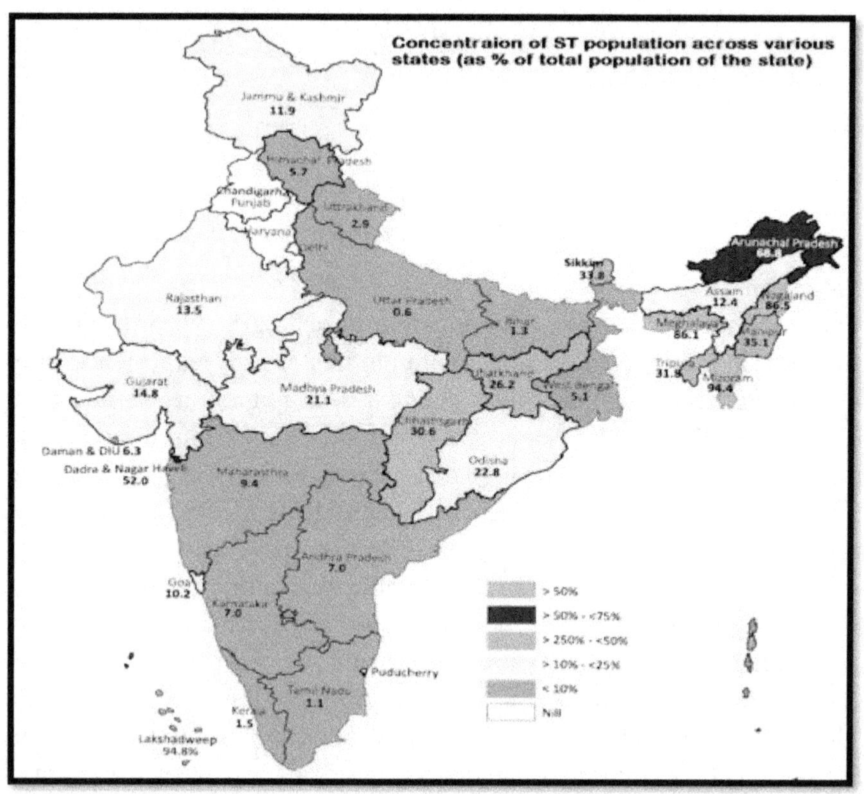

*Source:*vikaspedia.in

Impact of COVID-19 on Tribes

In response to the COVID-19 pandemic, India announced a sudden 21-day lockdown on 24 March, which was extended subsequently and lasted until 31 May 2020. The pandemic and the lockdown severely affected the livelihoods, health, and mobility of tribal peoples in India, who are referred to as Adivasis (original inhabitants)/tribal people in parts of the country, or as Scheduled Tribes in the Constitution of India. Indigenous peoples in India also continued to face a threat to their rights to land and identity, as several incidents of forced eviction were reported during the lockdown. (Press Release 17 June 2020)

The important impact of the Covid 19 pandemic on Indian tribal people are mentioned below:

Lockdowns Effect on Tribal Livelihoods: The effects of the pandemic and lockdowns on the livelihoods of tribal people in the country also varied from region to region and occupation to occupation. According to the Ministry of Tribal Affairs estimates about 1.5-2 million tribal people from tribal areas work across different parts of the country. With lockdown measures leading to suspension of manufacturing and service sectors activities, many workers were laid off or did not receive salaries. In the absence of social security, this led to widespread financial distress among migrant informal sector workers, including tribal migrants.

Tribal Marginalisation Threat: Livelihood and income losses were not the only way in which the pandemic led to further marginalisation of already marginalised tribal communities. While the sudden announcement of lockdown measures left them without their usual sources of income, the resulting financial insecurity had knock-on effects on the safety, health and education of these communities.

Impact of Covid pandemic on Sale of Forest Produce: Huge numbers of tribal people are estimated to be involved in the collection and processing of kendu leaves and beedi making. Kendu leaves and sale seeds provide tribals with a good amount of income even in the lean agricultural period and support them to invest in agriculture activities. Since the lockdown period coincided with the collection period (April–June) of MFPs, the tribals were unable to collect and sell their produce because of physical distancing norms, lack of buyers, and movement restrictions. The closing of local haats to avoid crowding deterred their sales and in the current situation traders are unwilling to buy MFP.

Deprive of Tribal Service Providers: The Tribal women have work as service providers to sections of society leading a more sedentary life. They work as agricultural labourers or domestic help. The women get some income by selling fresh milk to the local people. However, during the lockdown there was a sudden decline in the consumption of milk as people felt that consumption of open or unpacked milk could be unsafe. Therefore, some of them preferred packed milk and this change affected the basic earnings for the milk sellers. Consumption of meat and eggs also declined which affected the earnings of women from animal-keeping and pastoral groups. Their stigmatisation was also worsened because they were perceived by locals as "outsiders." Tribal and nomadic women who used to travel to different villages and sell their products or provide different services to villagers were stigmatised and labelled as coronavirus carriers. Many nearby villagers did not allow them to enter the villages in the lockdown period as they are strangers and coming from outside.

Tribal Women Vendors Faced Income Losses: The pandemic, adversely affecting the lives and livelihoods of the urban tribal women vendors who operate from them (many of whom are intra-state migrants). The tribal women vendors from being stationary market vendors resorted to street vending again during the lockdown, hence facing the ordeal of constant flight from authorities. The various strategies women vendors adopted included: vending in front of their rented house, street alleys, through mobile contact and delivering vegetables and fruits. Even with these coping strategies and the reopening of markets later, the incomes of the women vendors fell. The tribal market women vendors mostly rely on vegetable produce in the rural hill district areas, which is often supplied by rural women and farmers. Since the lockdown, supply chains have taken a hit and vendors are faced with shortages of steady supply of produce due to restrictions imposed on public transport leading to hike in prices of produce. There is a lack of customers due to the "stay home" advice, government restrictions, and short duration of lockdown relaxation, all leading to loss in profit.

Tribal Faced Violence and Dispossession: The slogan of "stay home, stay safe," which was also rendered meaningless in the context of various tribal groups who were not permitted to return to their homes. Though they could protect themselves against the virus, they were in danger from wild animals, snakes, scorpions and many other poisonous insects in the darkness. Yet they were not afraid of the difficulties and dangers of living in a hilly terrain but were more worried about a new beginning without any resources.

Instead, there are various instances where the state itself can be held responsible for dispossession of tribal lands A large number of land claims of these tribes and forest dwellers are mostly rejected, pending or limited rights are recognised by the states. Often, claimants are not even informed of the rejection order and any further chances for appeal. This trend has continued under cover of the pandemic. During the lockdown, instances of forestland diversion defied this act, where the environment ministry had given clearance to 11 projects across the country and issued new guidelines for relaxing forest and environmental clearance norms for mining by new leases (MoTA 2020). Some of these projects that required forest diversion were allowed without consulting the gram sabhas.

Healthcare Infrastructure of Tribes and Covid Pandemic: Tribal areas have an overall shortfall of 21% of sub-centres, 26% primary health centres (PHCs), and 23% community health centres (CHCs). Similarly, vacancies in tribal area PHCs are as high as 28% for doctors and 22% for nurses at PHCs and CHCs.These shortages are exacerbated by high rates of non-functionality of the health centres, absenteeism of personnel and unavailability of basic drugs and equipment. Currently, even the existing personnel are reassigned duties in COVID-19 hotspot regions causing a delay in regular medical treatment. Low immunity and the absence of healthcare facilities have severely limited their capacity to deal with the COVID-19 outbreak posing a serious threat to this population.

Poor Education Accuses for Tribal Children: Another social indicator that has been adversely impacted by the pandemic and lockdowns is education. The tribal children used to go to the ashram schools (residential schools) which were established in tribal areas. These children were getting free education, tuition, textbooks and other stationery, proper meals and shelter and scholarships. Due to the lockdown all these schools are shut. Schools in urban areas are at least trying to provide online education, but the schools in villages are lacking all the facilities. The economic calamity because of the lockdown has meant that they are dropping out even before completing school especially girls. This is leading to rising social insecurity, rising economic challenges and child marriages.

Tribals Face Mental Injustice: The COVID-19 pandemic has been a period of double emergency for the NT-DNT communities worsening their mental justice, which has anyway been historically violated. In this pandemic, it has been possible for mainstream society to stay at home because of being digitally connected, being able to work from home, etc. This sudden emergency created immense mental distress for the Indian tribals, creating a situation of double emergency. This is because till today, these communities are living in an emergency created by the scarcity of primary resources. They have now been faced by this additional calamity of the coronavirus pandemic. This community does not have a culture of storage and hoarding, because they are nomadic. They need to live light because they need to pick up everything they own and move to the next spot. Therefore, it was observed during relief operations that they did not have any ration stored at home. In this constant migration, and with no television, radio or other media, they did not even get any news about the pandemic. It is clear that the injustice faced by marginalised tribal communities is rooted in the mainstream globalised structures that have systemically excluded these communities.

Government Initiatives: The Ministry of Tribal Affairs, Government of India, announced some measures to provide relief to Tribal communities affected by the lockdown. These included the distribution of ration (subsidized food grain) kits to tribal families, provision of masks, soaps, gloves, and Personal Protection Equipment (PPE), purchase of existing available stock of tribal products from tribal artisans, and providing working capital and liquidity for tribal artisans, among others. To support indigenous peoples and forest gatherers who are dependent on forest produce for sustenance and income, the government increased the Minimum Support Price (MSP) for 49 Minor Forest Produce items and also included 23 additional Minor Forest Produce items in the Minimum Support Price List. Despite these measures, the central government's primary economic relief package to provide relief during the pandemic lacked any mention of tribal peoples/Adivasis.

Concluding Observation: The Indian government needs to more enforce public health policies in partnership with tribal people while respecting their traditional perspectives on diseases and their treatments. Officials in general are reluctant to work in remote forest areas so young officers, educators, and health professionals need to be trained to sensitize the tribal culture so that they can work exclusively to resolve their concerns. Given the lack of data on the tribal groups, a coordinated effort by various government and non-government agencies to monitor COVID-19 in the tribal communities is highly recommended. However, the efforts need to be adapted to the community to be effective rather than trying to integrate the community into the broader society, which will be counterproductive. Above all, the government must provide special budget allocation to ensure the public health safety for the often ignored and socially-suppressed indigenous communities while retaining their self-governance with minimal outside influence.

Reference

- Power, T., Wilson, D., Best, O., Brockie, T., Bearskin, L. B., Millender, E., & Lowe, J. (2020). COVID-19 and Indigenous Peoples: An imperative for action. Journal of clinical nursing.
- Agoramoorthy, G., & Hsu, M. J. (2021). COVID-19 and India's vulnerable indigenous populations. American Journal of Human Biology
- .https://www.epw.in/engage/article/covid-19-and-tribal-communities-how-state-neglect
- COVID-19 and Indigenous peoples, United Nations (https://www.un.org/development/desa/indigenouspeoples/covid-19.html)
- See, Press Release, 'Over 13,500 People Forcibly Evicted in India During the COVID-19 Pandemic: Need for an Immediate Moratorium on Evictions,' Housing and Land Rights Network, 17 June 2020. Available at: https://www.hlrn.org.in/documents/Press_Release_Evictions_COVID19_June_2020.pdf
- Carroll, S. R., Akee, R., Chung, P., Cormack, D., Kukutai, T., Lovett, R., ... & Rowe, R. K. (2021). Indigenous Peoples' Data During COVID-19: From External to Internal. Frontiers in Sociology, 6, 62.
- Impact of Covid-19 Outbreak and Lockdown Measures on Tribal and Forest Dwellers (Preliminary Assessment Report)https://www.fra.org.in/document/COVID-19%20Assessment%20Report.pdf
- How the Lockdown has Hit Tribal Communities and Forest-dwellershttps://thefederal.com/the-eighth-column/how-lockdown-has-hit-tribal-communities-and-forest-dwellers/

CHAPTER FIVE

Covid Vaccine and Curruption

*Dr. Archana Deshpande,**Kanishka Tomar,***Souman Debnath*

Abstract

Since late 2019, the coronavirus disease (COVID-19) outbreak has killed over four million people. Different vaccinations have been produced and delivered throughout countries to lessen the human and economic effects of COVID-19. The immunization of persons against COVID-19 has varied significantly among countries. We focus on public corruption in this analysis to explain the major reason for cross-country heterogeneity in vaccination progress. We believe that, after adjusting for other relevant predictors of immunization progress, nations with a greater level of governmental corruption have had less success in the vaccination of their populations.

Introduction

On March 11, 2020, the World Health Organization (WHO) proclaimed the SARS-CoV-2 (COVID-19) outbreak a pandemic. Since then, the epidemic has raged on, with worldwide morbidity and fatality rates continuing to rise. This emphasizes the need of creating and guaranteeing access to inexpensive, safe, and effective vaccinations, as well as their timely and equitable distribution. Following the favorable findings released by a number of vaccine candidates in November 2020, vaccinations have been authorized at an unprecedented rate in various regions of the world. Governments will need to act quickly to guarantee that their citizens have access to safe and effective COVID-19 vaccinations. Many nations have stated their intention to establish COVID-19 immunization programmes that will cover their whole populations. As a result, the scope and complexity of vaccine allocation, distribution, and prioritizing will be unprecedented. The R&D Blueprint, a worldwide strategy, and readiness plan has been activated by WHO to enable for rapid activation of research and development operations during epidemics. It aims to speed up the development of COVID19 diagnostics, vaccines, and therapeutics by improving collaboration between scientists and global health professionals, speeding up the research and vaccine development process, and establishing new norms and standards to learn from and improve the global response. The WHO secretariat has also examined and published a collection of current WHO guideline papers pertaining to the development, production, and evaluation of COVID-19 vaccines. Current WHO guidelines may give important direction and information for the development, manufacture, and assessment of prospective COVID-19 vaccines, according to the listing. A COVID-19 vaccination should be considered a worldwide public utility. To ensure that people have equal access to vaccinations, governmental institutions should identify and resolve any possible gaps and impediments, such as the danger of corruption in vaccine distribution and allocation procedures. In times of crisis, combating corruption is a top concern. This point was reaffirmed in the Secretary-Statement General's on Corruption in the Context of COVID-193 in October 2020, when Antonio Gutierrez stated, "(corruption) is much more devastating in times of crisis – as the world is witnessing now with the COVID-19 epidemic." He also pointed out that the epidemic is opening up new avenues for corruption.

This policy study discusses possible corruption risks associated with the deployment of a COVID-19 vaccination and how these risks might be addressed to help public institutions in times of crisis. For these efforts, the United Nations Convention against Corruption provides a robust worldwide foundation.

Corruption Risks

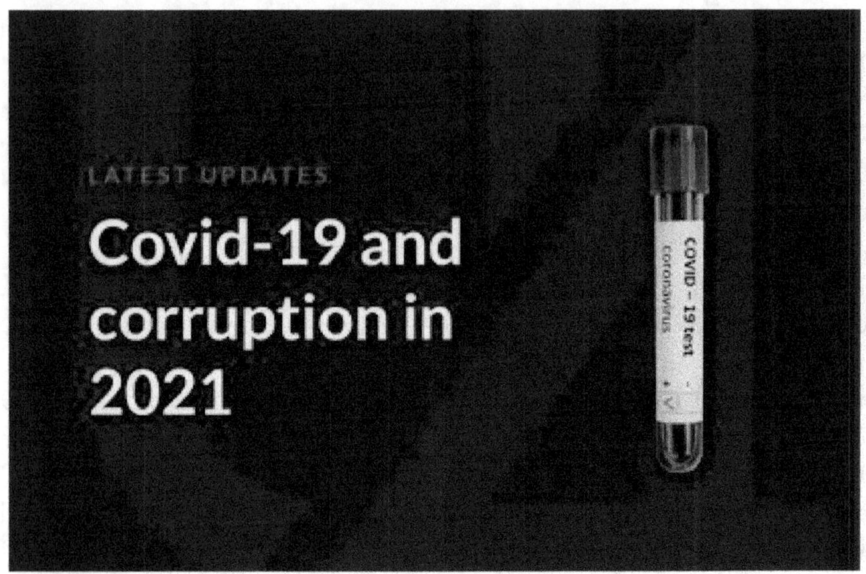

Source: coe. int

The dangers include theft and corruption, as well as the weaponization of vaccinations.While most vaccinations have minimal street value, the initial scarcity of a COVID-19 vaccine, along with the likelihood of strong demand from fearful communities, will make it a target for theft and diversion.

Many countries lack what the WHO deems to be well-functioning and integrated pharmaceuticals regulatory systems, making it more probable for inferior and fraudulent vaccines to reach the market. These might have disastrous consequences, stoking doubt and distrust, intensifying the pandemic, and eventually killing lives.

Add to it the genuine possibility that vaccinations may be used as a new weapon by powerful governments to exert geopolitical influence. The Russian Sputnik V vaccination has already piqued the curiosity of over 30 countries. Russia authorized the vaccine in August, ahead of phase 3 testing, in a decision that some have criticized as premature and motivated by nationalism rather than science.

Any vaccination that is approved and deployed too soon risks causing more harm than benefit, and not only to the receiver; has a lack of transparency in vaccine development and approval allowed skeptics to discredit vaccines. However, the fact that this vaccine piqued the curiosity of so many countries before specifics of its safety and efficacy were revealed — demonstrates how concerned governments are about not having enough supply or access.

It also erodes trust in government institutions. Institutional distrust might lead to vaccine hesitation and a drop in vaccination coverage, expanding the vaccine gap even more. Furthermore, an increase in the demand for forged vaccination certificates and illegally obtained vaccines might set off a vicious cycle of vaccine injustice and corruption.

Corruption Makes Vaccination Difficult For The Most Vulnerable.

"We have a scenario presently where high-income nations are offering booster dosages," Jonathan Cushing, Transparency International's Head of Global Health, said, "but the reality for many people throughout the world is very different."

One of his main points was that transparency and fairness within countries have taken numerous forms, ranging from allegations of nepotism in Sweden and many other countries to calls for payments for immunization in Uganda. The bribe sums asked in SEK or Euro are little, but when compared to daily income in Uganda, for example, the bribes are substantial, according to Cushing.

Because of the scarcity of vaccinations in LMICs, individuals are ready to rely on personal ties to obtain immunizations. As vaccination restrictions become more stringent, Transparency International has received instances of people seeking to circumvent the system by purchasing vaccine certificates without being vaccinated in order to return to work and earn a living. This might be due to a vaccination scarcity or vaccine reluctance. Dr. Hans Kluge, WHO Europe Director, told a news conference in early December that vaccines should not be made mandatory "until you have first gone out to the people."

The race to create a COVID-19 vaccination is heating up. COVID-19 research and development have received significant governmental and commercial funding because of the necessity of creating a vaccine, medicines, and diagnostics. A significant portion of this effort has gone into developing a worldwide COVID-19 vaccination that is both safe and effective. The World Health Organization is keeping track of the enormous number of vaccine candidates undergoing human clinical trials as well as experimental vaccines being tested on animals. Vaccine research and development is a time-consuming and expensive process that can take up to a decade to complete — with no guarantees of success. Processes have been accelerated under the present emergency scenario, and many vaccine candidates are showing promising results in clinical testing, with the first ones having already been licensed for public use and others nearing completion.

The early research phase, the patent application, the preclinical testing phase, the three phases of clinical trials, and the registration procedure are all part of the research and development process. Shortcuts in any of these phases can result in serious health hazards and a loss of public trust in the vaccine's advantages. There are several examples of how the research and development process for the COVID-19 vaccine is being accelerated.

Governments are also granting or preparing to issue emergency use licenses, including filing for the WHO's Emergency Use Listing. The rapid speed of research and development, as well as the pressing need for a vaccine, may open the door to corruption, which would stymie public health initiatives. Conflicts of interest8 associated with the funding of COVID-19 vaccine research and development are one example of corruption risk. A high-level officer of a government's COVID-19 vaccine research and development programme, for example, who previously worked for a private vaccine company that is bidding for a large contract under the government's programme to manufacture a vaccine candidate, could be involved in the contract's decision-making process. Some governments have established special commissions to negotiate the procurement of COVID-19 vaccines with laboratories and institutions doing vaccine research and development. There is a possibility of corruption in what these agreements involve if there is a lack of openness. As part of their agreements with the special commissions to acquire a vaccine for the populations9 of high-income nations, these laboratories and universities have frequently been required to sign secrecy statements. Such agreements risk jeopardizing low-income nations' access to a COVID-19 vaccination on a global scale. Vaccine deployment and distribution methods that are either ineffective or non-existent Strong supply mechanisms will be required for the successful deployment of COVID-19 immunisation programmes. These systems must ensure proper vaccine storage, handling, and stock management, as well as stringent temperature controls throughout the supply chain and the upkeep of sufficient logistics management information systems. This is critical in order to protect the COVID-19 vaccination supply and avoid any disruptions from manufacture to service delivery.

Throughout the vaccination deployment process, there is a possibility of corruption. Vaccines, for example, might be taken from the public supply chain and sold on the illicit market or held for personal use throughout the transit process. If there are no trustworthy supervision methods in place, vaccine supplies are also at danger until they reach the hospital or public health center giving the shots. Vaccines may also be stolen by public health facility employees for sales on the black market or in their own private operations. When supplies are limited and demand is strong, as during a pandemic, this danger becomes even greater.

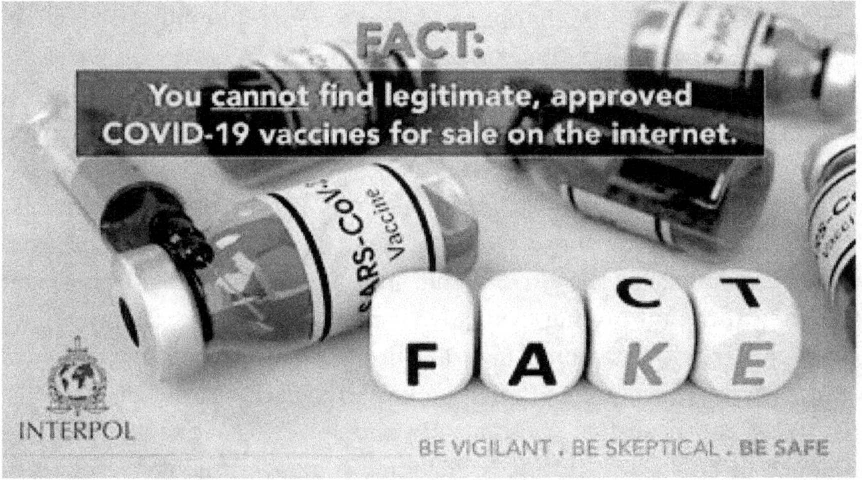

Source: Interpol.int

The procurement of vaccines might be tainted by corruption. Under normal conditions, the public procurement process is one of the most vulnerable areas of government to corruption. Because of the massive amounts of money involved in public procurement, it is extremely prone to corruption. Public procurement is projected to account for 15–30 percent of the gross domestic product in several nations.

Purchase scandals are common, but the procurement of medicines and medical devices is particularly vulnerable to corruption in the healthcare industry. Throughout the procurement process, there is a possibility of corruption. Corruption risks during the pre-bidding process include predicting demand for a product or service incorrectly, evading tender rules, and customizing tender papers to favor a certain bidder. During the bidding process, there is a danger of bribes or kickbacks from suppliers being paid to government officials, as well as collusion and market split among bidders. Such restricted networks thrive because of their exclusion, and this is amplified when speed and fast effect are exchanged for monitoring. Finally, corruption risks in the post-bidding process include misleading invoicing, altering contract clauses, and failing to deliver bought vaccinations.

The urgency of the demands, the necessary flexibility, and the expected speed all increase the potential of corruption in procurement during a public health crisis. This might open the door to more individual discretion, thereby increasing the possibility of corruption. Many governments have granted direct contracts without going through a competitive process, making it difficult to ensure that measures are in place to identify and prevent corruption and misuse.

Unscrupulous government officials may use the procurement process to profit themselves or those close to them by demanding bribes from vendors. Providers, on the other hand, may take advantage of shortages to demand exorbitant pricing from government buyers and cooperate with other suppliers. Governments may acquire poor or fraudulent products if vendors pay government officials to get around regulatory regulations, jeopardizing the health of their people and lowering citizens' faith and confidence in public institutions - including the government's reaction to the epidemic.

Risks of corruption with emergency financing

Large sums of money are allocated to quickly treat a crucial and complicated problem during a crisis response. The International Monetary Fund estimates that around US$ 11 trillion has been given internationally as fiscal support to the COVID-19 response as of June 2020. 19 The World Bank's Board of Executive Directors also approved US$ 12 billion in October 2020 for poor nations to fund, buy, and distribute COVID-19 vaccines (as well as testing and treatments) for their populations.

If sufficient due diligence mechanisms are not in place, large inflows of funds that are paid fast may be prone to corruption. During the Ebola virus disease outbreak in Sierra Leone, for example, the Sierra Leone Audit

Service discovered a lack of documentation underlying nearly US$ 3.3 million in payments from the government's Ebola-directed accounts, as well as US$ 2.5 million in disbursements with incomplete documentation. Many instances of apparent fraud and corruption were also identified in the Audit Service's report, including in the procurement of supplies and payments for Ebola response personnel.

Due to fraud and collaboration in the Ebola response, the International Federation of Red Cross and Red Crescent Societies is reported to have lost millions of dollars. Sierra Leone had an increase in maternal death rates during the Ebola virus outbreak. Sequential mixed-methods research undertaken from October 2016 to January 2017 verified and expanded on the explicit and causative association between corruption and maternal death rates in Sierra Leone. Women who had given birth during the Ebola epidemic showed suspicion of health-care personnel, according to household surveys, owing to fees asked for health treatment that would normally be free. As a result, women were disproportionately impacted by the Ebola outbreak and its aftermath.

Nepotism/favoritism in access to vaccines

A billion individuals are projected to be dispersed populations with no recognised identities, mostly in developing nations. When a COVID-19 vaccination becomes available, reaching these people will be very difficult. Because COVID-19 vaccine supplies will be limited in the early phases of deployment, governments must guarantee that the vaccine is distributed properly and that each dosage reaches its intended recipient. Corruption issues, such as conflicts of interest and nepotism, are also present in decision-making connected to vaccine allocation to priority groups. For the allocation and prioritizing of COVID-19 vaccination, the concepts of equal regard, reciprocity, and legitimacy indicated in the WHO Strategic Advisory Group of Experts on Immunization (SAGE) values framework should be implemented early on in their distribution and allocation. Transparency — access to information about government decision-making – is crucial in this case. Transparency makes it easier to detect corruption and reduces the risk of it occurring. Transparency removes barriers to information and allows for examination and monitoring. Governments must guarantee that the criteria used to designate priority vaccination recipients are transparent and that this information is widely disseminated to the public. Transparency is also critical in ensuring that people are informed about how, where, and when to get vaccines.

Source: himalmag.com

Vaccine policy choices those are corrupt

The business sector, as well as other interested parties, may try to influence government vaccination policy and deployment decisions. Payoffs and bribes from a firm having a stake in which vaccination is acquired, for how much, from whom, and where it is delivered might make government officials vulnerable. Individuals with close links to the health industry may also be involved in the vaccine purchasing and deployment decision-making process. As an example, a physician serving on a national immunization technical advisory board may promote a vaccine candidate created by a corporation that has paid her/him with research or consulting funds without disclosing the conflict of interest.

Measures to reduce corruption risks

In light of these major hurdles, Member States should consider the following immediate and long-term reaction steps to identify and reduce corruption risks that might jeopardize public access to safe and effective COVID-19 vaccinations. The only legally binding, worldwide anti-corruption instrument is the United Nations Convention against Corruption. It establishes a worldwide framework and crucial instruments to promote accountability, integrity, and transparency during and after the COVID-19 epidemic.

Domestic retaliation measures should be implemented as soon as possible.

A special committee will be in charge of emergency finances and vaccination distribution.

Source: istockphoto.com

During a public health emergency, the establishment of a dedicated committee with a strong anticorruption mandate to oversee the prioritizing, distribution, and monitoring of vaccination programmes, as well as associated public policy, can serve as a key oversight body. Its capabilities should include the capacity to track emergency fund disbursements, vaccine purchases, vaccine distribution, and associated operations in "real-time," allowing any red flags to be discovered and resolved swiftly.

Vaccine procurement that is transparent and responsible during a pandemic, open contracting and e-procurement can help create transparent and accountable public emergency procurement processes. Because it informs the public about who is buying what, from whom, and at what price and quantity, open contracting may be beneficial in decreasing corruption.

Furthermore, e-procurement has the potential to reduce corruption. It enables for the public distribution of pertinent data, such as contract bidding and awarding, via a dedicated website, ensuring that the aspect of transparency is maintained. During times of crisis, public procurement procedures can also assist improve openness and limiting the danger of purchases from illegal vendors. The European Union has produced a guideline sheet on possibilities and flexibilities for purchasing products, services, and works connected to the COVID-19 pandemic under its public procurement system. Colombia's national procurement agency is checking vendors that have signed a framework agreement with the country.

To reduce the danger of corruption, use secure storage and dissemination mechanisms. For the safe delivery of COVID-19 vaccines and to reduce the possibility of vaccines being diverted from public supply to black markets, secure storage and distribution mechanisms are essential.

Vaccine manufacturers are already working on measures to avoid vaccine theft. This might involve things like storing vaccinations in secret areas, using a Global Positioning System tracking system to track supplies in route and using "dummy" vehicles to throw criminal networks off. Hospitals may need to increase the security of the rooms where COVID-19 vaccinations are housed.

Conduct risk assessments for corruption

A corruption risk assessment can be used by public organizations to detect corruption vulnerabilities within their operations and design efficient, cost-effective solutions to eliminate those vulnerabilities or risks, if possible and ideally before extensive vaccination distribution. Potential corruption risks during COVID-19 vaccine distribution procedures will be mitigated by timely corruption risk assessments within health ministries or agencies charged with vaccine procurement and distribution. State of Integrity: A Guide to Conducting Corruption Risk Evaluations in Public Organizations, published by the UNODC, can be used as a starting point for assessments. This book enables a customized strategy to identify vulnerabilities and corruption threats, as well as mitigation strategies.

Long-term solutions

Increasing the effectiveness of anti-corruption laws and programmes COVID-19's fast expansion has forced governments to act promptly and nimbly, underscoring the significance of having effective anti-corruption mechanisms in place. This might involve revising and improving current anti-corruption laws and policies to ensure that they promote measures like active civil society engagement, preserving the rule of law, and guaranteeing effective public-sector management. Furthermore, governmental institutions, particularly those involved in the production, distribution, and allocation of COVID-19 vaccinations, should have measures in place to improve their openness and responsibility to the people they serve.

To monitor the distribution process and verify acceptable receipts, comprehensive auditing, supervision, accountability, and reporting procedures are in place.

Conclusion

Any COVID-19 vaccine will be deployed with tremendous financial resources over the world. To maintain accountability and successfully limit corruption concerns, these financial resources will require robust audits, supervision, and reporting methods. In the Philippines, emergency legislation established a Joint Congressional Oversight Committee, which requires the President to report to Congress on the allocation and utilization of money committed to combating the COVID-19 outbreak on a weekly basis.

References

- https://www.unodc.org/documents/corruption/COVID-19/Policy paper on COVID-19 vaccines and corruption risks.pdf
- https://www.bmj.com/content/374/bmj.n1724
- https://ti-health.org/content/is-covid-19-vaccine-nationalism-corruption/
- https://www.wionews.com/photos/covid-corruption-and-scandals-that-rocked-the-world-395815
- https://www.transparency.org.uk/coronavirus-covid-19-vaccine-equitable-distribution
- https://www.u4.no/topics/covid-19-and-corruption
- https://fortune.com/2021/08/14/covid-vaccine-corruption-distribution-rollout/
- https://www.google.com/ search?q=corruption+of+covid+vaccine&rlz=1C1DFOC enIN659IN659&source=lnms&tbm=isch&sa=X&ved
- =2ahUKEwjI9pqnsKn1AhU24HMBHU39BKwQ AUoAXoECAEQAw&biw=1366&bih=657&dpr=1
- https://www.nature.com/articles/s41598-021-02802-1

Social Media and Mental Health During the Outbreak of COVID-19

*Sheuli Das,**Tanvir Ahmed Mondal

Abstract:

The pandemic of Coronavirus Disease 2019 (COVID-19) has resulted in a global health crisis that has had a profound impact on our perceptions of the world and our daily lives. People utilise social media platforms to communicate information in a variety of settings. During the COVID-19 outbreak, preventing the spread of rumours and disinformation is critical, because misinformation and fake news cause panic, worry, and anxiety in people, predisposing them to a variety of mental health problems. In this paper, the researcher tries to emphasis the users' activity on social media platforms during the COVID-19 health emergency and mental health to understand the whole scenario.

Keyword: Mental health, Social media, Pandemic, Covid-19, SARC-COV-2, Mental disorder.

Introduction:

In 2019, SARS-CoV-2 was first discovered infecting humans. It's thought that the virus spreads from person to person via droplet emitted when an infected person coughs, sneezes, or talks.On March 11, 2020, the World Health Organization declared COVID-19 a global pandemic. The new coronavirus is an infectious respiratory illness that is spread from person to person like the flu, but with a lower mortality rate than SARS, MERS, and H1N1.

At this time, little is known about COVID-19, which understandably causes anxiety and distress, especially among those of us who suffer from anxiety disorders.

We think now is a good time to hit the pause button and remind ourselves that resilience and hope (and even humour!) can be just as contagious as panic-buying (a.k.a. toilet paper hoarding) and frequent handwashing.

The most prevalent observation on computed tomography imaging of the chest was bilateral lung involvement with ground-glass opacity. According to the US National Institutes of Health, It was first discovered in the city of Wuhan, Hubei Province, China. It is the successor to SARS-CoV 1, the virus that caused the SARS outbreak in 2002–2004. As described by WHO (2019), Working from home, temporary unemployment, home-schooling children, and a lack of physical interaction with other family members, friends, and coworkers are all new realities that require us to take care of our mental as well as physical health for this time .

Media Coverage of Natural Disasters and Mental Health

Despite the importance of the media in disseminating critical information during times of mass trauma, numerous studies have suggested that disaster media exposure can lead to negative mental health outcomes. Early 9/11 and Iraq War-related television exposure, for example, has been linked to an increase in posttraumatic stress (PTS) symptoms (Silver et al., 2013). Following the Boston Marathon bombings, individuals outside the directly affected community were found to have higher acute stress symptoms after six or more daily hours of bombing-related media exposure (Holman, Garfin, & Silver, 2014). Those who were frequently exposed to distressing media images reported a higher risk of posttraumatic stress disorder (PTSD) 6 months later nurses fighting COVID19 among adolescents who did not experience the Sichuan earthquake in 2008.(Yeung et al., 2018). Although disaster media exposure has been shown to have negative effects on a variety of psychological outcomes (see Pfefferbaum et al., 2014), secondary traumatic stress (STS) has not been adequately addressed (BenZur, Gil, & Shamshins, 2012; Blanchard et al., 2004). As a result of being indirectly exposed to traumatic events, STS causes PTSD-like symptoms such as arousal, avoidant behaviours, and intrusive imagery (Branson, 2019; Ludick & Figley, 2017). Given that the majority of people do not have SARSCoV2, it is critical to consider whether media exposure is linked to STS in the general population. Indeed, Li et al. (2020) discovered that the general public experienced even more vicarious trauma than frontline workers.

Source: bbc.com

The DSMM proposes three response states (cognitive, emotional, and excitatory states) as mediator mechanisms between media use and health outcomes. Only two studies specifically looked at the mediating process, using acute stress and fear as mediators (Holman, Garfin, Lubens, & Silver, 2019; Silver et al., 2013). Silver et al. (2013) found that acute stress did not mediate the link between media exposure and physical health in longitudinal studies, whereas Holman et al. (2019) discovered that fear of future terrorism significantly mediated the link between media usage and functional impairment in longitudinal studies. Although understudied, there is some evidence that negative affect may mediate the effects of disaster media.

The COVID19 Stressor's Moderator Role

Disaster-related stressors, in addition to media exposure, have been identified as one of the most important predictors of mental health (Paul et al., 2014). In the current study, the COVID19 stressor was operationalized as a common stressor that people experienced during the pandemic. A higher disaster stressor level was linked to poor mental health outcomes. Prior research has found that people who have been exposed to more disaster-related stressors are more likely to develop DSMIV anxiety mood disorders (Galea et al., 2007). Furthermore, social media use was linked to depression only when the COVID19 stressor was high (but not low).

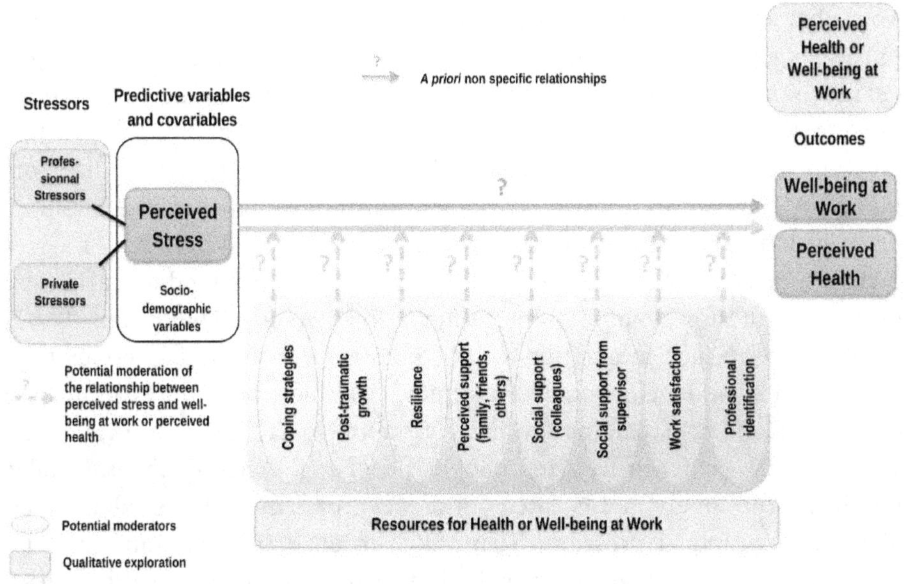

Source: bmjopen.bmj.com

It appears that people who were exposed to a higher level of stress were more susceptible to depression. It should be noted, however, that the interaction term makes a minor contribution.

Collective trauma victims had higher levels of physiological arousal and fear, and many of them continued to be concerned about themselves and their families (Pfefferbaum et al., 1999). Excessive exposure to social media coverage is likely to have maintained their heightened reactivity to traumatic events, potentially predisposing them to develop post-disaster stress. However, the interaction of social media use and the COVID19 stressor was only significantly associated with depression, not STS or anxiety, which is somewhat surprising.

One possible explanation is that people who have been exposed to the COVID19 stressor have real problems, such as a lack of necessities or bereavement. Immersion in social media may not solve the problems, but it may exacerbate their feelings of helplessness and sadness. Depression, in this sense, may be a more common symptom of distress than other psychological symptoms.

Review of literature :

Many of us use social media sites like Facebook, Twitter, Snapchat, YouTube, and Instagram to locate and communicate with one each other in this society. The online world has altered drastically in the previous two years. Young men and women may now exchange ideas, thoughts, personal information, images, and videos at an incredible rate and thanks to the creation of social media (Wang & Liang,2011) . its ultimate impact on many performance indicators have become an almost indispensible element of daily living in today's culture (Rapp et al.,2013).While each has its own set of advantages, it's vital to realise that social media will never be a substitute for genuine human interaction (Asur & Huberman,2010). It takes face-to-face interaction with others to release the hormones that relieve stress and help you feel happier, healthier, and more optimistic (Hong et al.,2021).Spending too much time on social media, ironically for a technology supposed to bring people closer together, can instead make you feel more lonely and isolated—and exacerbate mental Disorder issues like anxiety and depression. (Guntuku et al.,2019). The uncertainty surrounding the pandemic has resulted in a variety of mental health issues.

Methodology and Scope of the study:

Tries to understand the significance of Social media and Mental health during the outbreak of COVID-19 in present context . It is a descriptive study. The qualitative aspects of the research study were also taken for consideration. This study is completely based on the secondary data. A systematic review was done in detail for the collected literature. Secondary sources of data used are journals, reports, documents, company websites and scholarly articles,PubMed,Google Scolar and other academic publications .

Present Result of Social media and Mental health during the outbreak of COVID-19:

Social media can allow people to precipitate social change on massive scales.It Seek or offer emotional support during tough times (Griffis et al.,2014).We now have access to more information than ever before thanks to social media,but there are both positive and negative consequences to our use of this technology (Akram & Kumar ,2017).Here, we look at some of the benefits and drawbacks of social media use, as well as the impact it can have on our mental health during the covid -19.

Negativeness:

When used with bad intentions, social media has the capacity to achieve significant beneficial change, but it may also have negative consequences.

* Twitter and other social media platforms can be hotbeds for spreading harmful rumours, lies, and abuse that can leave emotional scars.

* Sharing endless photos and your deepest thoughts on social media can lead to an unhealthy sense of self-centeredness and a disconnect from real-life relationships.

* web-based social networking promotion's ramifications

* Individuals with serious mental illness who utilise social media may engage in more communal and civic activities.

Positiveness:

According to a (2018) University of Pennsylvania study, reducing social media use to 30 minutes a day resulted in a significant reduction in levels of anxiety, depression, loneliness, sleep problems, and FOMO.

Communicate and stay up to date with family and friends around the world.

Consulting Doctors online anywhere and anytime

More data available to health researchers

Access to information in developing regions

Social media provides a collaborative environment for seemingly unlimited numbers of people to communicate socially.

It requires in-person contact with others to trigger the hormones that alleviate stress and make you feel happier, healthier, and more positive.

Conclusion:

Social media value on covid and mental health concious ,new policy of social media. Exposure to COVID-19 information acts as a stressor during this epidemic, activating cognitive processes and increasing ruminative thinking (Michl et al,2013). social media has become an important part of the lives of many individuals living with mental health. Many of these people utilise social media to share their experiences

References:

* Asur, S., & Huberman, B. A. (2010, August). Predicting the future with social media. In 2010 IEEE/WIC/ACM international conference on web intelligence and intelligent agent technology (Vol. 1, pp. 492-499). IEEE.
* Hong, W., Liu, R. D., Ding, Y., Fu, X., Zhen, R., & Sheng, X. (2021). Social media exposure and college students' mental health during the outbreak

of CoViD-19: the mediating role of rumination and the moderating role of mindfulness. Cyberpsychology, Behavior, and Social Networking, 24(4), 282-287.

- Guntuku, S. C., Buffone, A., Jaidka, K., Eichstaedt, J. C., & Ungar, L. H. (2019, July). Understanding and measuring psychological stress using social media. In Proceedings of the International AAAI Conference on Web and Social Media (Vol. 13, pp. 214-225).
- Thakur, A. (2020). Mental health in high school students at the time of COVID-19: A student's perspective. Journal of the American Academy of Child and Adolescent Psychiatry, 59(12), 1309.
- Guelmami, N., Khalifa, M. B., Chalghaf, N., Kong, J. D., Amayra, T., Wu, J., ... & Bragazzi, N. L. (2021). Development of the 12-Item Social Media Disinformation Scale and its Association With Social Media Addiction and Mental Health Related to COVID-19 in Tunisia: Survey-Based Pilot Case Study. JMIR Formative Research, 5(6), e27280.
- Ruffolo, M., Price, D., Schoultz, M., Leung, J., Bonsaksen, T., Thygesen, H., & Geirdal, A. Ø. (2021). Employment uncertainty and mental health during the COVID-19 pandemic initial social distancing implementation: A cross-national study. Global Social Welfare, 8(2), 141-150.
- Saha, K., Torous, J., Caine, E. D., & De Choudhury, M. (2020). Social media reveals psychosocial effects of the covid-19 pandemic. medRxiv.
- Goel, A., & Gupta, L. (2020). Social media in the times of COVID-19. Journal of Clinical Rheumatology.
- Li, L., Zhang, Q., Wang, X., Zhang, J., Wang, T., Gao, T. L., ... & Wang, F. Y. (2020). Characterizing the propagation of situational information in social media during covid-19 epidemic: A case study on weibo. IEEE Transactions on Computational Social Systems, 7(2), 556-562.
- Cuello-Garcia, C., Pérez-Gaxiola, G., & van Amelsvoort, L. (2020). Social media can have an impact on how we manage and investigate the COVID-19 pandemic. Journal of clinical epidemiology, 127, 198-201.
- Michl, L. C., McLaughlin, K. A., Shepherd, K., & Nolen-Hoeksema, S. (2013). Rumination as a mechanism linking stressful life events to symptoms of depression and anxiety: longitudinal evidence in early adolescents and adults. Journal of abnormal psychology, 122(2), 339.
- Wang, Q., Chen, W., & Liang, Y. (2011). The effects of social media on college students. MBA Student Scholarship, 5(13), 1548-1379.
- Rapp, A., Beitelspacher, L. S., Grewal, D., & Hughes, D. E. (2013). Understanding social media effects across seller, retailer, and consumer

interactions. Journal of the Academy of Marketing Science, 41(5), 547-566.

- Griffis, H. M., Kilaru, A. S., Werner, R. M., Asch, D. A., Hershey, J. C., Hill, S., ... & Merchant, R. M. (2014). Use of social media across US hospitals: descriptive analysis of adoption and utilization. Journal of medical internet research, 16(11), e264.
- Akram, W., & Kumar, R. (2017). A study on positive and negative effects of social media on society. International Journal of Computer Sciences and Engineering, 5(10), 351-354.

CHAPTER SEVEN

Issues and Challenges of COVID 19 on rural economy in West Bengal

**Ratan Shil

Introduction

The COVID-19 pandemic is the greatest global humanitarian challenge the world has faced since World War II. The virus has spread widely, and the number of cases is rising daily as governments work to slow its spread. West Bengal had moved swiftly, implementing a proactive, nationwide, many labels of lockdown, with the goal of flattening the curve and using the time to plan and resource responses adequately. India's effort to combat the COVID-19 virus with a vaccinated policy has been praised over the globe. However, the lockdown came with an economic cost and cascading impact on all the sections of society. The Covid-19 induced lockdown in West Bengal has a huge economic shock. It started across the country on 24 March 2020 and is still ongoing as a new form Omicron with restrictions. It stalled the economy with complete closure imposed on enterprises across all sectors. Even though agricultural activities were exempted, in the initial phases of the lockdown the agriculture value chain also faced large-scale disruptions. This had a seriously detrimental effect on the rural Indian economy. The coronavirus pandemic has also triggered a massive reverse migration from the urban to rural areas in large parts of the country.

Agriculture and Economic over View in West Bengal

West Bengal is the primary business and financial hub of Eastern India. The state is primarily dependent on agriculture and medium-sized industry.

West Bengal has the Jute industry, Tea industry. West Bengal is rich in minerals like coal. Since the independence of India, The Green Revolution bypassed the state. Rice and potato are considered to be the principal food crops. The state is the largest source of the important food crop of rice, a staple diet across India, with an annual output of around 16.1 million tonnes in FY 2015–16, and the second-largest producer of potatoes in India with an average annual output of 11 million tonnes in FY 15-14 West Bengal is also the second-largest fish producing state. Apart from these, jute, sugarcane and wheat are the top crops of the state. Other major food crops include maize, pulses, oilseeds, wheat, barley, and vegetables. Tea is another important cash crop. Darjeeling is globally recognised for the tea plantation of the acclaimed Darjeeling tea variety.

As per the state budget presented in the state legislative assembly on 24 June 2016, West Bengal's nominal GSDP at current prices has risen to INR 9.20083 trillion or US$140.68 billion in the year 2015–16, the average INR to US$ exchange rate in that year being INR 65.4. West Bengal's average population in that year being 95.5 million, per capita nominal GSDP at current prices for the economic year 2015-16 can be calculated as US$1473. In West Bengal every economic activity has been vastly infected by COVID 19 Pandemic.

Economic Statistics of West Bengal (2020–21)

GDP growth	**8% (2020–21)**
GDP per capita	**115,348 (US$1,500) (2020–21)**
GDP by sector	**Agriculture: 21% Industry: 26% Services: 53%**

Source: As per the Government Report

Issues and Challenges

COVID-19 brings crisis on several economic and non-economic fronts over the globe. There would be demand and supply shocks because of trade restrictions and labor mobility. In India, there would serve consequence on 81 percent of people employed in the informal sector (ILO, 2018). Almost 90 percent of the workers in west Bengal have survived with no minimum wage or any kind of social security (Sharma, 2020). Even after the unorganized worker's social security act (2008), only 5-6% got enrolled for social security. The return or reverse migration amid the agrarian crisis in the agricultural sector from urban to rural areas pose big challenges to the rural economy. The specific issues are:

1. **Return or Reverse Migration:** According to International Migration Organisation (2011), "return migration is the act or process of going back to the point of departure, is the returning of people to their origin or place of habitual residence after spending some time at another place".

- It can be a voluntary return or forced migration. Irrespective of the reason for migration, the return poses a significant impact on the demography, society and economy of rural areas. The reverse migration significantly impacts population size and characteristics over the period. It is very hard for people to integrate from society amid fear of contamination from the virus.
- Finally, return migration to rural areas has a significant impact on the economy of the rural areas as well since in some cases it dramatically contributes towards boosting the economic activities in the area.

Field realities show migrant labours are higher in the case of UP and Bihar followed by MP, Punjab, Rajasthan, Uttarakhand, Jammu and Kashmir, and West Bengal. Currently, returnees are coming with empty hands which have left their destination to save their life from poverty and hunger. All the workers in West Bengal in the informal economy are at the risk of falling deeper into poverty during the crisis.

Source: https://www.google.com/

1. **Agrarian Crisis and Reverse Migration**: There is a crisis in the agriculture sector over the past two decades. In India, especially West Bengal the majority of farmers are small landholders facing the problem of falling productivity, water scarcity, Product value, etc. The majority of the returnees were marginal farmers in the past. Due to Covid 19, the reverse migration will increase pressure on agriculture which is already overburdened.

2. **Fall in Producer and an increase in the consumer price**: Due to the Corona crises the reverse migration will further result in to fall in the producer price of crops which will reduce farm wages and income. On the other hand, due to low productivity and hoarding of food articles, there will be a rise in the prices of food items which will majorly affect poor people.

3. **Rural Unemployment and Poverty**: Rural employment and the economy is fully destroyed by the impact of the Corona pandemic.

Reverse migration, a fall in producer price and increasing pressure on the agricultural sector will lead to an increase in rural unemployment and poverty. During the third wove of Covid 19 rural employment and poverty levels are decreasing day by day in West Bengal.

4. The threat **of the Health System:** Due to the under-reporting of cases because of low testing, there is the fear of the outbreak of COVID-19 which can cause mass mortality. stile now rural population in West Bengal are not properly aware of COVID-19. Hence, there is a need to prevent the health system in both urban and rural areas from being overburdened and stop community spread.

Future Challenges and Policies

Our central and state government has announced various packages and policies to resolve the impact of Covid 19. The major focus of the package is land, labour, liquidity and laws which will cater needs of cottage industries, MSMEs, labourers and middle class. In the long run, to reduce inequalities of income, regional imbalance and share of migrant workers, localization of industries and employment is the need of the hour. Apart from providing credits, there is also a need to work on institutional factors such as law and order, corruption etc. for effective implementation of the policies. In the manufacturing industry, migration or migrant labourers are the engines of growth. In COVID-19 or post COVID world there would be always a demand of manufacturing goods. Therefore, the government has to work on the mechanism of how these migrant labours are brought back to their respective jobs.

The localization of industries and employment can release pressure from the agricultural sector. There should be a comprehensive plan for structural transformation from the primary to the modern sector. Agricultural reforms such as competitive credits, modern farm inputs and better producer prices to be taken to make agriculture profitable. In short run, measures such as cash incentives should be given to the migrant laborers and marginal farmers to save them from poverty and starvation. Similarly, wage subsidies should be given an informal sector. Above all, mass corruption in the system is the biggest challenge in the effective implementation of plans.

Conclusions

In the present coronavirus pandemic also, the immediate challenge was the restoration of the supply chains for essential commodities as well as reducing the plight of the distressed migrant worker. The government, through its various interventions specifically through the Prime Minister Garib Kalyan Yojana and MNREGA has provided timely relief to migrants in these difficult times. While most of the challenges presented by the pandemic have been efficiently handled it is also important to make use of the opportunities the crises provide. A case in point is the new opportunity the crisis has thrown open in the agriculture supply chain network. In many parts of the country, FPOs stepped in successfully creating supply chains in the COVID scenario. There are also numerous examples across metros in the way groups of farmers took the initiative to ensure direct delivery of products to gated communities and societies for products ranging from exotic avocados to perishables like regular fruits and vegetables. The entire logistics chain has been set in motion, but it currently lacks depth and width. An institutional fillip required which builds on this with expertise can generate livelihoods at various levels.

References

- Mondal, B. K., Sahoo, S., Paria, P., Chakraborty, S., & Alamri, A. M. (2021). Multi-sectoral impact assessment during the 1st wave of COVID-19 pandemic in West Bengal (India) for sustainable planning and management. Arabian Journal of Geosciences, 14(23), 1-26.
- Singh, B. P. (2020). Impact of COVID-19 on rural economy in India. Available at SSRN 3609973.
- Pratap, B. (2020). Impact of COVID-19 on Rural Economy in India. Munich Personal RePEc Archive: New-Delhi, India
- Rawal, V., Kumar, M., Verma, A., & Pais, J. (2020). COVID-19 lockdown: Impact on agriculture and rural economy. Society for Social and Economic Research.
- Rahaman, M., Roy, A., Chouhan, P., Das, K. C., & Rana, M. J. (2021). Risk of COVID-19 Transmission and Livelihood Challenges of Stranded Migrant Labourers during Lockdown in India. The Indian Journal of Labour Economics, 64(3), 787-802.
- Modak, T. S., Baksi, S., & Johnson, D. (2020). Impact of covid-19 on Indian villages. Review of Agrarian Studies, 10(2369-2020-1852).
- https://en.wikipedia.org/wiki/West_Bengal

CHAPTER EIGHT

Global Politics on Covid-19 Vaccine: Changes and Issues

**Sk Abdul Shahid

Introduction

After almost two years since the virus entered our lives, we still do not know how to extricate ourselves from the crisis.The outbreak of Covid-19 pandemic has been themost disastrousconsidering the other pandemics in therecent past. Preparedness of public health care systemand social awareness about the basic health care amongthe people both have been brought to the forefrontduring this crisis episode. In view of the moderncapitalist systems across the countries it has beenobserved that public health care system was neverprioritized by the State machinery all over the world.Hence, the State's response to the crisis was a mix ofpanic and haphazardly undertaken measures to controlthe spread of the virus.The dire need for a Covid 19 vaccine made thecountries to make heavy short-term arrangements formedical infrastructure and R&D expenditure. Theeconomic and social upheaval during the crisis andlockdown worsened the situation and the politicaleconomy aspects were atfunction in case of the medicaltrials for such vaccine. The intellectual property rightsfor medical inventions, international treaties for medicalhelp and medicinal exchange, domestic concerns ofincreasing Covid-19 cases and the issue of maintainingsocial harmony recapitulate the lockdown episodes inmany countries.

Vaccine is seen as a beacon of hopefor billions of us. However, the unpleasant reality is that the availability of vaccineand vaccine nationalism are becoming the fundamental challenges for an equitableand legitimate distribution of it because currently, just a handful of COVID-19vaccines have been developed, mostly by a few medically advanced countries.[1] Hence, production, distribution, and delivery are falling waybehind the global demand.The demand-supply imbalance has led to a rise in "vaccine nationalism" whereby "even before the end of final stage human trials or regulatoryapproval, several wealthier countries like Britain, France, Germany and the UShave entered into pre-purchase agreements with Covid-19 vaccine manufacturers.This implies that countries are averse to share their stocks of vaccines with othercountries until vaccination against the virus is complete in their own country.[2] Of course, vaccine nationalism poses a predicament insolving this global problem. Though prioritizing themselves seems to increasetheirprotection and vulnerability to the virus but the reality is ifeverybody is not safe, nobody is safe.

The rich countries purchase and hoardsupplies of the vaccine for their utilization. Therefore, thevaccine manufacturing countries are planning to lock it by patent. Though voicesare getting stronger for deglobalization and withdrawing within borders, thispandemic has given the lesson that it is impossible to be secure in a country unlessthere is security in all of them.[3]

Even the United States has not committed to sharing vaccines with any countrybefore vaccination of the American people is complete. Many other countries thatwere supposed to export vaccine to their allies blocked the export. The countriesthat cannot develop a vaccine and dismantle the pandemic are in an extremelytough position. The question here is this: how can states navigate the internationalsystem to eradicate the virus in the world ultimately, and how can they do itwithout compromising their national interests? Vaccine diplomacy might be theanswer.

Diplomacy at the moment sounds like a critical force in solving vaccinedistribution and delivery.[4] This means the state leaders,policymakers, and diplomats should handle the vaccine issues. However, theeffectiveness of diplomatic task often depends on several factors, such as howstrong is the relationship between the incumbent and the export countries; howgood (proactive, fast, objective, determined in advancing state's national interestsand ready to finance etc.) are the diplomats of the incumbent countries innegotiating issues. For example, the Russian vaccine Sputnik V hasbeen registered in 39 countries, mainly those once in the Soviet sphere ofinfluence in sub-Saharan Africa and Latin America. Still, it has also beenregistered to two European Union member states. Thus, vaccine diplomacyappears to be an effective tool for many countries at the moment of the Covid-19crisis.

A vaccine to change the world

The question is: can a vaccine change the course of the current crisis? Can we restore the equilibrium we have lost? It seems that no one, at least not in the scientific or decision-making community, has doubted it. In the same way that the crisis was announced, from the time the global consequences of the virus started to be discerned in January 2020, a scientific race began in a frantic and unprecedented search for the magic bullet that would halt the epidemic. Long before the new coronavirus appeared, vaccines have been the most cost-effective strategy in the health arena. In other words, they are the cheapest strategy for preventing diseases in terms of achieving the best results on a grand scale. A study by Johns Hopkins University in 2016 showed that for every dollar invested in immunisation in the 94 countries with the lowest income in the world, their health systems saved US\$16. Without risk of exaggeration and in the absence of a detailed study, when this analysis is applied to COVID-19 and the most advanced economies –where the virus is having the greatest effects– this return may be multiplied by hundreds or thousands of dollars for every one invested in vaccines. Bearing in mind the estimates of the World Bank, the worldwide contraction in the economy due to the pandemic accounts for over 5% of GDP, or, in comparative terms, the worst recession since the Second World War and three times more severe than the crisis of 2008. Vaccines, viewed as the only tool that can provide herd immunity as a means of starting to dismantle barriers, such as the restrictions on movement, social distancing and commercial closures, are worth their weight in gold.

Hence the race to obtain the magic bullet. Hence the unprecedented investment –mainly from the public purse– to secure an effective vaccine as quickly as possible. Since the first cases of COVID-19 emerged in Wuhan on 31 December 2019, only 11 days elapsed before the genetic sequence of the new coronavirus was published and just one month later, on 7 February 2020, the first prototype of a vaccine for use on humans in clinical trials was finalised. Never before in human history had there been so much haste to obtain a vaccine. There were only 333 days between the publication of the genetic sequence and a British woman, Margaret Keenan, receiving on 8 December in a hospital in Coventry the first regulated vaccine approved for distribution, once the results of the clinical trials had been published. The Pfizer and Sputnik V vaccines –the vaccine developed in Russia– and the Chinese Sinovac vaccine were available before this, but with limited authorisations and restricted to emergency use in their countries. Never before had a vaccine been developed in so short a time. It took 18 years to develop the first flu virus in the previous century; for other more recent diseases such as AIDS, the search is still continuing more than three decades later. Not surprisingly, therefore, the speed with which the vaccine was obtained raised doubts in many people. But the research work on which the first generation of vaccines is based has been carried out for more than a decade in trials to address other diseases, such as cancer; with the emergence of COVID-19, attention has switched to attacking the new coronavirus specifically. The massive injection of resources made it possible.

This unprecedented scientific race has not only been effective in providing a vaccine in record time, it has also managed to procure not one but various vaccines and to multiply production such that they are delivered in sufficient quantity. From the outset, securing the vaccine was the goal of all the great world powers: China, Russia, India, the US and the EU. Obtaining it first would lend not only a strategic advantage in terms of international relations and selling it on almost a global scale, but also international prestige at a time of shifting leadership. Courtesy of this open competition, in the first week of January 2021 there were more than 80 vaccines undergoing human trials, 20 of them in their final phases, seven of them so far approved for limited use and three approved for distribution and unlimited use.

The race does not end with obtaining a vaccine, however. Once its safety and efficacy has been ascertained it has to be produced on a large scale. The challenges posed by the pandemic require an extraordinary volume of vaccines to be manufactured. If all the vaccines require two doses, as is the case with the first to be approved, 15 billion doses would be needed to immunise the entire population of the planet, a figure that the largest manufacturer in the world, the Serum Institute of India, regards as impossible to attain in less than four years. There are limiting factors in the capacity to build new production plants and the scalability of the Pfizer and Moderna vaccines, based on a new technology platform, for which there is insufficient knowledge among the producer countries. There are alsoproduction problems affecting critical components, such as the vials used for the safe shipping of vaccines that in some cases have to be stored at less than -70°C, a temperature lower than polar winter. Another factor is that the most risk-averse producers do not set about manufacturing doses of their vaccines until they have obtained authorisation. Unless it is assured of a market, private capital does not invest. The responsibility and above all the will to pass from the development phase to distributing the vaccine among the population as quickly as possible was thus immediately transferred to the political agenda and togovernments, which, given their inability to halt the virus by other means, decided to accept the risk of remitting funds to the producers and starting to manufacture millions of doses while the vaccines were still being tested in the trial phase.

Vaccine and global security

Since the beginning of the pandemic, the collective voice that we have heard wasthe necessity for vaccine inventions. The vaccine should not be administered onlyin a pocket of countries. Instead, it should be made available and reached out toall countries and all the people. Hoarding and locking vaccine by patent andnationalism have been the fundamental barrier to reaching out to billions who needthe vaccine most. Hence, the world is witnessing the least developed countries'governments fighting to win the vaccine battle. Who wins and who loses in thebattle depends on who is powerful financially and has good relationshiphistorically?contends that the historical and modern-day accounts of the vaccineand vaccine diplomacy are remarkably great. However, these have not taken anoverarching framework for its expanded role in foreign policy. Vaccine diplomacyas the branch of global health diplomacy relies on the use or delivery of vaccines".[5] In the diplomatic battle to get the vaccine, it is important toremindessential of Edward Jenner, who discovered the smallpox vaccine in1798,[6] on how to administer the smallpox vaccine. Vaccinediplomacy should be premised on the spirit of Louis Pasteur's remarks that"science knows no country, because knowledge belongs to humanity.[7] Hotel (2014; 2006) and Franklin (2020)reminded that Dr Albert Sabin (developer of the oral polio vaccine) travelled fromthe US to the Soviet Union during the Cold War to collaborate with Sovietvirologists on prototype development for the oral polio vaccine.[8] The success was possible because they placed humanity overideology for joint scientific cooperation.Vaccine diplomacy grew in popularity in the later half of the twentieth century.

Vaccines were used to negotiate so-called 'days of tranquillity'— UNICEF, oftenin partnership with WHO, uses this method to ensure that children have access tohealth care during times of conflict— in over a dozen nations in the 1980s and1990s, including Afghanistan, Angola, Chechnya, the Democratic Republic of theCongo, El Salvador, Guinea Bissau, Iraq, Lebanon, the Philippines, Sierra Leone,Sri Lanka, and Sudan. Under the auspices of WHO, in 2007,Romania, Vietnam, Serbia, Brazil, Iran, Thailand, Republic of Korea, Mexico,Egypt, Indonesia and India collectively received US$25 million that aimed tobuild their influenza vaccine production capacity through technology transfer. The2010 survey reported 12 million influenza vaccine doses were produced by theeleven manufacturing countries, with three of them successfully implementedvaccine production and distribution countrywide.[9] It is alsoworth noting a relatively low-profiled China humanitarian response, alongsideothers, the United States, France, Sweden, Norway, and Switzerland, against theEbola outbreak in West Africa in 2014-2015.[10]

These are remarkable examples of how vaccine administration should go about.Historical instances of global health led to an unprecedented collaboration whichhas some impact on today's diplomacy. For example, vaccines became integratedas critical tools in helping developing nations and international efforts to ensureuniversal access for low- and middle-income countries" are also fostering greatercollaboration. The Global Vaccine Action Plan (GVAP) is also critical. Endorsedin May 2012 by World Health Assembly, it is working to provide more equitableaccess to existing vaccines to all populations by 2020 — based on the premise thathealth is a fundamental human right.

COVID-19 Vaccine and diplomacy

As we entered the COVID-19 period, we realized how a pandemic could wreakhavoc on global normalcy. The World Bank (2020) estimatesthat due to the pandemic, from 88 to 115 million people will fall into extremepoverty in 2020, with the totalrising to as many as 150 million by 2021. Theeconomic cost of COVID-19 (which is expected to reach between US$5.8 andUS$8.8 trillion globally— almost 6.4–9.7% of global GDP) (Chowdhury andChakraborty, 2021). More than 500 million full-time jobs are estimated to be lostfrom the job market.[11] These stark changes will affect the globaleconomy, population mobility and foreign policy.A race for the invention of a magic bullet that would halt the epidemic began soonafter the outbreak came to be known to us. Now the race is to obtain the magicbullet, i.e. vaccine. Governments have spent at least €93 billion on COVID-19vaccines and therapeutics globally since the beginning of the pandemic.[12]

Hence the unprecedented investment to secure an effective vaccine asquickly as possible. Never before in human history had there been so much hasteto obtain a vaccine. Never before had a vaccine been developed in so short a time.It took 18 years to develop the first flu virus in the previous century; for othermore recent diseases such as AIDS, the search is continuing more than three decades later.On the geopolitical front, there is vaccine diplomacy and vaccine nationalism. Theformer is demonstrated by swift action to build COVAX Facility after thedeclaration of COVID-19 as a pandemic. COVAX convenes Gavi, the VaccineAlliance, WHO, and a Coalition for Epidemic Preparedness Innovations (CEPI)to support the development, manufacture, or distribution of new COVID-19vaccines. It emphasizes equity access for low- and middle-income countries(LMICs).[13]

India currently hostssome of the largest vaccine producers, which now work with WHO forprequalification and COVAX for financing and distribution.At the same time, vaccine nationalism has steadily gained geopoliticalsignificance as high-income nations led the global race to secure vaccineaccess for their populations, leaving behind the vulnerable ones in thegeopolitical competition. The politics of aid and mask diplomacy that dominatedthe international relations in the first year of the COVID-19 pandemics have beenreplaced by vaccine nationalism and distribution, which "all, of course, act as anextension of existing geopolitical competition".[14] The USGovernment refused to participate in COVAX, withdrawing from WHO and the'America First' executive order in December 2020 to secure a "priority access"for COVID-19 vaccines.[15]

The Brexit row worsened due toan EU's blockade against the vaccines produced by EU manufacturers to NorthernIreland. Compared to 49 wealthy countries that administered 39million vaccine doses, only 25 million doses were delivered to one developingcountry. In addition, vaccine producers in Russia and China test orapprove vaccines of uncertain quality, so far avoiding stringent regulatoryauthorities yet negotiating bilateral agreements with Latin American, Asian, andAfrican nations to sell vaccines or propose joint production.

Conclusions

A patent waiver could also be the way to achieve equitable vaccine access globallywithout being dependent upon vaccine diplomacy. The suspension of the IPprotections on Covid-19 vaccines allows producers to export raw materials,industrial parts and components and allow technical knowledge transfer fromvaccine makers in the global north to new manufacturers in the global south.[16] There are needs to be aware of immediateimplications and limitations once the waiver is enforced, including raw materialand supply bottleneck, infrastructural and manufacturing limitations and fundingunavailability. However, in the long run, waiving the patentcould end "the vaccine apartheid".[17]Weaker nations are falling behind in global vaccine competitions. But the migrantcommunities who are already in vulnerable conditions bear the brunt of thiscompetition disproportionately. Migration is becoming an increasingly essentialaspect of bilateral and international diplomatic relations, just as it is in war andpeace, trade, economics, culture, the environment, and human rights. Despite agrowing bodyof research on the many dimensions of modern diplomacy,migration has yet to be included in such studies, despite its prominence inpractitioners' plans. This is not to suggest that research into the relationshipbetween foreign policy and population movement has not been done. Indeed, thereis a substantial body of knowledge in this domain, with the majority of it focusingon immigration across OECD countries.While taking on the rewarding role of global vaccine leader may appear to have ashort-term benefit, it is in the national interests of the world's wealthiest countries.Nonetheless, it is unlikely to see the pandemic ending anytime soon unless theytake on this responsibility. Therefore, policymakers and leaders in all affluentcountries, particularly the most powerful states, should reject vaccine nationalism,and promote vaccine diplomacy as a top priority.

References

- Krasnyak, Olga. (2021). From vaccine nationalism to vaccine diplomacy.https://www.olgakrasnyak.com/post/from-vaccine-nationalism-tovaccine-diplomacy.
- James Darwin and N Lagman. (2021). Vaccine nationalism: a predicament in endingthe COVID-19 pandemic, Journal of Public Health, Volume 43(2):e375–e376, https://doi.org/10.1093/pubmed/fdab088.
- Peterson S. (2002). Epidemic disease and national security. Security Studies12:43–81.
- Krasnyak, Olga. (2021). From vaccine nationalism to vaccine diplomacy. https://www.olgakrasnyak.com/post/from-vaccine-nationalism-tovaccine-diplomacy.
- Hotez PJ. (2020). Anti-science extremism in America: escalating and globalizing.Microbes Infect 22(10):505-7.

- Bazin H. (2000). The Eradication of Smallpox: Edward Jenner and the First andOnly Eradication of a Human Infectious Disease. New York: AcademicPress. 246 p.
- Hotez PJ. (2021). Preventing the Next Pandemic: Vaccine Diplomacy in a Timeof Anti-Science, Johns Hopkins University Press.
- Kaufmann JR, Feldbaum H. (2009). Diplomacy and the polio immunizationboycott in northern Nigeria. Health Affairs 28: 1091–1101.
- Friede M, Palkonyay L, Alfonso C, Pervikov Y, Torelli G, Wood D, Kieny MP.(2011). WHOinitiative to increase global and equitable access toinfluenza vaccine in the event of a pandemic: Supporting developingcountry production capacity through technology transfer, Vaccine, 29,Supplement 1, A2-A7.
- Huang, Y., (2017). China's response to the 2014 Ebola outbreak in West Africa.Global Challenges, 1(2): 1600001.
- Ullah AKM Ahsan, Nawaz F and Chattoraj D. (2021). Locked up underlockdown: The COVID-19 pandemic and the migrant population, SocialSciences & Humanities Open, 4.
- Hoecklin Madeleine. (2021). €93 Billion Spent by Public Sector on COVIDVaccines and Therapeutics in 11 Months. https://healthpolicywatch.news/81038-2/.
- Excel, JL., Saville, M., Berkley, S. et al. (2021). Vaccine development foremerging infectious diseases. Nat Med 27, 591–600 (2021).https://doi.org/10.1038/s41591-021-01301-0.
- Grgic Gorana. (2021). The international politics of the pandemic.https://www.ussc.edu.au/analysis/the-international-politics-of-thepandemic.
- WHO. (2020). 172 countries and multiple candidate vaccines engaged in COVID-19 vaccine Global Access Facility.
- Gonsalves, G., &Yamey, G. (2021). The covid-19 vaccine patent waiver: Acrucial step towards a "people's vaccine". The British Medical Journal,373: n1249.https://doi.org/10.1136/bmj.n1249.
- Byanyima W. (2021). A global vaccine apartheid is unfolding. People's lives must come before profit. Guardian. 29 January 2021.https://www.theguardian.com/global-development/2021/jan/29/a-globalvaccine-apartheid-is-unfolding-peoples-lives-must-come-before-profit

Global Politics and Covid Vaccine

*Tanwangini Sahani,**Dr.Abhishek Srivastava*

Introduction

The global effort to develop and distribute an effective vaccine for the COVID-19 coronavirus disease has yielded several safe and effective options a year after the pandemic began. The development of multiple vaccines at such a rapid pace is unprecedented; typically, the process takes eight to fifteen years.

However, challenges remain, including dangerous new strains of the virus, such as omicron; global competition over a limited supply of doses; and public scepticism about the vaccines.

The world confronts major vaccination shortages as the COVID-19 pandemic spreads. Nations are still grappling with a mechanism for guaranteeing equitable vaccination delivery after 170 million diagnoses, over 3.5 million fatalities, and eighteen months. The vaccination project's current situation is concerning, as the vaccine availability gap between industrialised and underdeveloped countries continues to increase day by day.

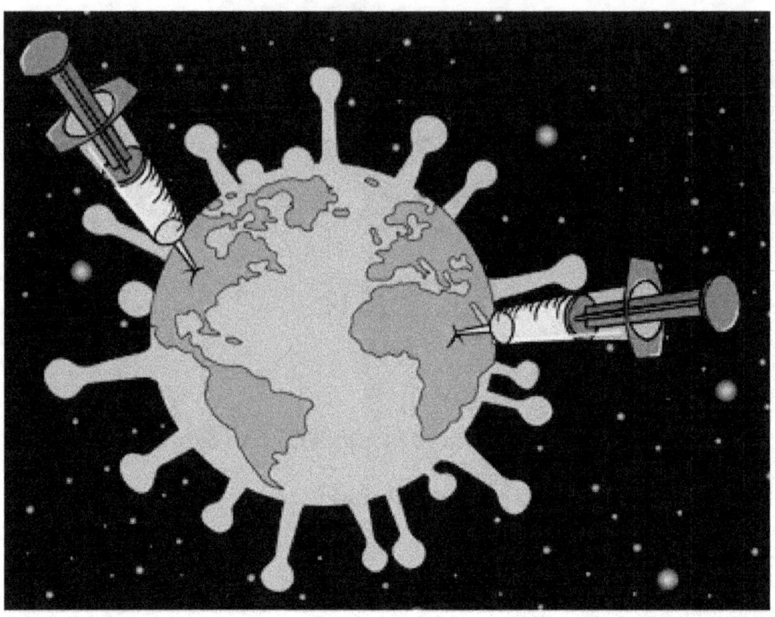

Figure 1: www.eiu.com

According to Science magazine, rich and middle-income countries received roughly 85 percent of the total doses provided till May 25, 2021. Global vaccination attempts have been hampered by great power politics, which have jeopardised international efforts to make vaccines more accessible. Despite being a commendable international attempt for greater worldwide availability, the COVAX initiative has run into problem after problem. The vaccine supply is coagulated: the majority of vaccines are produced in the West, whereas India and Russia struggle to scale up production, and the efficiency of Chinese vaccines is debatable. The lack of raw materials, big-pharma profiteering, and pharmaceutical lobbies that passionately favour intellectual property controls over vaccinations at the expense of human health and survival are exacerbating the problem.

In countries like India, where the emergence of the delta strain and eased restrictions resulted in a disastrous surge in mid-2021 that slowed vaccine supplies elsewhere, unequal vaccination distribution was felt acutely. By the end of the year, the country had boosted its vaccination effort, immunising more than 500 million people. Meanwhile, the World Health Organization (WHO) has warned that the epidemic will be prolonged due to a lack of vaccine access in Africa, where less than 10% of the population has been properly vaccinated. Many countries have imposed or are proposing vaccine mandates in order to maintain development. COVID-19 immunizations are required for both government and private-sector personnel in Italy and Saudi Arabia, for example. The United States followed suit for its public sector and major private enterprises, despite legal challenges to the decision. Others have enacted mandates that apply only to healthcare personnel.

Objectives

- To understand the Hunt for a Waiver of Intellectual Property
- To know why Covax Collapsed
- To discuss India's Case study

Analysis and Discussion

The Quest for Intellectual Property Waiver

During the epidemic, India and South Africa asked the World Trade Organization (WTO) to suspend the intellectual property rights of COVID-19 diagnostic tools, treatments, and vaccinations. Without these specific steps, the reasoning goes, the wealthier countries will gain from new technology as they become available, while the less economically developed countries will continue to be plagued by the pandemic, with negative consequences for both.

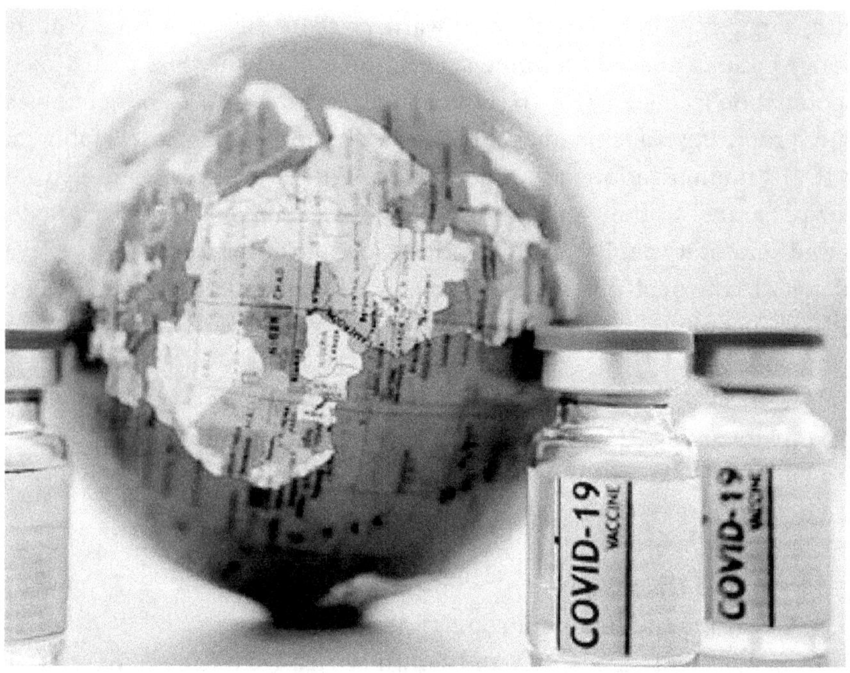

Figure 2: www.ei-ie.org

Intellectual property rights, such as patents, are blocking new medical items from becoming available and inexpensive, according to the suggestion. A temporary ban, it was said, would allow many countries to begin production earlier, rather than manufacture being concentrated in the hands of a limited number of patent holders, allowing for the quick scaling that was believed essential at the time. In May 2021, both countries restated the draught plan, which was backed by 62 countries.

Most developed nations are vehemently opposed to this waiver, claiming that deregulation of intellectual property rights would impede the manufacture and availability of high-quality vaccines. Furthermore, Western pharmaceutical companies claim that such a waiver will stifle research in the sector and impair vaccine quality. They also questioned developing-country pharmaceutical companies' technological capabilities to supply safe vaccines in sufficient quantities. The US has just decided to accept IPR waivers, but only for vaccines and only after a series of text-based talks. Opponents of the idea, on the other hand, have maintained their stance, claiming that "there is an ocean between this waiver request and what the US suggested." The EU is taking a tougher stance than the US, and has proposed an alternative that will make a temporary waiver agreement even more doubtful. This process, if it fructifies at all, is predicted to take years, negating the fundamental goal of addressing immediate vaccine dose requirements in the developing world. Long-term monopoly rents for western big pharma appear to have been sequestered by commercial concerns and self-interest.

The Collapse of COVAX

The most difficult aspect of the global vaccination campaign has always been securing vaccine supplies to disadvantaged countries. COVAX, a global programme to create a common pool of vaccines from which all countries would receive their part, was identified as the solution. It was carried out through an Advance Market Commitment (AMC), in which the rich world agreed to pre-fund their quota in order to share the expense of supplying free vaccines to underdeveloped countries. The quota for each country was established at 20% of the population, although this would be adjusted once all members had met their quotas.

If COVAX had remained the sole source of vaccine supplies for all countries, it would have worked. Rich countries, on the other hand, directly negotiated their quotas with pharmaceutical corporations while booking through COVAX as an insurance (for instance, the UK and EU signed deals for doses as much as three times their population). This resulted in a two-for-one situation. COVAX had funding constraints due to a lack of demand from wealthy countries. On the supply side, pharmaceutical companies gained money by selling dosages to wealthy countries and did not transfer enough of their stock to the COVAX pool. The vaccination supply chains got extremely clogged as a result of the lack of vendors. Low-income countries are the hardest hit, as they are heavily reliant.

India's Case Study

India's Prime Minister Narendra Modi took the first dosage of Covaxin — the country's own COVID-19 vaccine – on March 1, 2021, setting off phase 2 of the world's largest vaccination campaign. In January, India began immunising frontline workers, with the goal of vaccination 300 million frontline workers, health care professionals, and vulnerable individuals by August. The immunisation push occurs at a pivotal juncture in the country's history. COVID-19 infections are fast increasing in numerous Indian states, sparking fears that the country is on the verge of a second, more deadly wave of the virus. Despite the logistical and infrastructure hurdles of vaccinating India's enormous population, the country has received international accolades for its contributions to global vaccine production and supply initiatives.

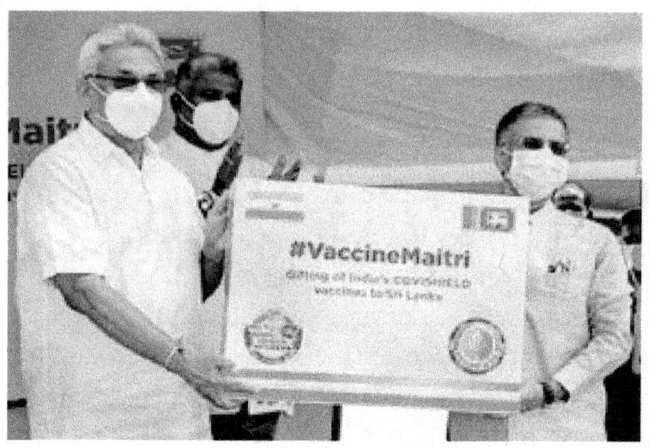

Figure 3: www.sundayguardianlive.com

India initiated the Vaccine Maitri (Vaccine Friendship) project in January 2021, which is a huge diplomatic endeavour to gift and supply made-in-India vaccinations to low-income and developing countries around the world. India, as the world's third-largest pharmaceutical manufacturer, is a strong contender in the race to develop COVID-19 vaccines. India's pharmaceutical industry is a global powerhouse, producing approximately 60% of the world's vaccinations, including vaccines for Diphtheria, Pertussis, Tetanus (DPT), Tuberculosis, and Measles. The Covishield vaccine (developed by Oxford University – AstraZeneca) is produced by India's Serum Institute, which is also the world's largest vaccine producer by volume, while Covaxin is produced by India's Bharat Biotech. Several more made-in-India vaccine possibilities, including a potentially game-changing nasal vaccine and Russia's Sputnik V vaccine, are in various phases of research.

Vaccines are substantially cheaper in India, even if they are not yet available on the commercial market and vaccine manufacturers are supplying doses to the government at subsidised costs. In addition to being less expensive, vaccinations manufactured in India are better suited to countries with a weak cold chain and infrastructure. Pfizer and Moderna vaccines must be kept at sub-zero temperatures, whereas both Indian-made vaccines can be kept at 2 to 8 degrees Celsius, or refrigerator conditions. India also has a lot of experience and expertise in mass immunisation campaigns, and its vaccine deployment is being keenly watched in other nations.

India's vaccine diplomacy on a global and regional scale

India's vaccine nationalism has taken a different turn as the world's largest producer of vaccines, or the 'Pharmacy of the World,' as popularised by External Affairs Minister Subrahmanyam Jaishankar (Das, 2021). The scientific ability to develop new vaccines has been used to establish national identity and as a marker of superiority. Indian pharmaceutical companies are major producers of vaccines that are distributed worldwide, particularly in low-income countries, supplying more than 60% of vaccines to developing countries. Despite having a strong manufacturing base and early access to Covid-19 vaccines, Indian companies are finding it difficult to produce enough doses to adequately manage the pandemic. The Serum Institute of India (SII), for example, is one of the most important pharmaceutical companies involved.

The world's largest vaccine manufacturer – currently engaged in the production of Covishield, a local name for the Oxford-AstraZeneca vaccine – has stated explicitly that the majority of its vaccine will be distributed to Indians before being exported. Despite this, reality appears to be moving in a different direction. India is a country that has enacted a reassuring vaccine policy India's Prime Minister has stated that the country's production of vaccines will be used for the benefit of all humanity in the fight against the Covid-19 virus. pandemic. India has pledged to help neighbouring countries with vaccines. Bhutan, the Maldives, Nepal, and Bangladesh received 'gifts' or grants in accordance with the agreement. 360 Niladri Chatterjee and colleagues with the 'Neighbourhood First' policy of New Delhi (Hindustan Times, 2021; Srivastava, 2021). Kay et al., 2021). Covishield vaccine doses have also been delivered in large quantities. Plans have been made to supply vaccines to Seychelles, Mauritius, and Myanmar. after regulatory approvals, to Sri Lanka and Afghanistan. Saudi Arabia, South Africa, Brazil, Morocco, Bangladesh, and India are among the countries that India supplies on a contractual basis. Myanmar. The United States has praised such action as "true courage." a pal' (Business Today, 2021).

The Covid-19 vaccine, the most recent and sought-after commodity in international diplomacy, gives India some clout with neighbours who are otherwise enamored of Chinese investments. China has been a tough competitor for India in recent years. With China's increasingly visible footprint in South Asia, it has increased its influence. Sri Lanka, the Maldives, Bangladesh, Nepal, Africa, and other countries Lacking the economic resources that China possesses, and India's attempts to match them, So far, exerting influence has been largely ineffective. In terms of international relations, As a result, one cannot blame India for exploiting her resources and engaging in diplomacy. even if it means extending her geopolitical diplomacy at a time of global health crises It is undeniable that India's vaccine gifts will help to polish its international image and earn it international respect. her goodwill, particularly in South Asia, where it is frequently chastised for its 'big brother' attitude behaviour.

The international world is concerned about 'vaccine nationalism' and the growing imbalance in vaccine supplies, hence India's vaccine diplomacy is timely. Many affluent countries have been chastised by the WHO for hoarding vaccines, leaving little for middle- and low-income countries. Many countries are turning to India to overcome the accessibility and availability gaps as they struggle to acquire supply. India is also in the forefront of efforts to level the playing field in vaccine development and supply, especially for developing countries. For the length of the pandemic, or until most nations have vaccinated their people, India and South Africa have applied to the WTO for an intellectual property waiver for COVID-19 vaccines and patents.

Beyond semantics and morality, India's vaccine diplomacy is a successful tool and instrument of Indian soft power and influence, cementing and deepening ties in India's neighborhood and the Indo-Pacific. For years, India has fought for a seat on the UN Security Council and has developed relationships with smaller developing countries, notably in the Indian and Pacific Ocean regions. India's vaccine diplomacy could result in crucial votes at a time when the country holds a non-permanent seat on the United Nations Security Council and is hosting the G20 conference in 2023. The goodwill that India has gained through its vaccination diplomacy may pay off in the future.

Recommendation and Findings

1. India, a vaccine powerhouse, has started providing its neighbours, including Nepal, Bangladesh, and Sri Lanka. Vaccines are increasingly being used as diplomatic weaponry by smaller countries.
2. Governments, multilateral organisations, and private companies have invested billions of dollars in the development of COVID-19 vaccines.
3. More than two dozen vaccinations have already been distributed, including those from Pfizer and BioNTech, Moderna, and Sinopharm, and roughly half of the world's population has been fully immunised.
4. Israel, which is known as the world's vaccine champion, has delivered doses to Honduras as well as the Czech Republic, which is intending to create a diplomatic mission in Jerusalem.
5. The United Arab Emirates has been assisting Gaza, a Palestinian region under Israeli blockade, and Tunisia with targeted funding.
6. China, which was ahead of the game with mask distribution at the outset of the pandemic, has been delivering vaccines to other countries, often for free.
7. However, due to its limited industrial capacity, Russia has been forced to split the spoils of rising global power with China.
8. Serbia has risen to the top of continental Europe's Covid immunisation rankings thanks to Beijing's assistance.
9. China and Russia's vaccine diplomacy has covered the supply gap left by the West and India. The immunizations' dependability has long been questioned.

Conclusion

Vaccines have become another weapon of global geopolitics and a component of what some have dubbed "global nationalism" to use in geopolitical conflict. While people in developed countries are vaccinated at a rate of one dose per second, people in developing and less developed countries are still waiting for their first vaccine. Higher-income countries are primarily motivated by their technology and intellectual property monopolies in vaccine research, as well as an emphasis on speedy economic recovery, owing to increased economic competitiveness with China. Due to unanticipated vaccine shortages in India, the country has had to not only use its excess capacity for internal consumption but also import more vaccines to protect its population against a virulent second wave. As a result, the "Vaccine Maitri" initiative has been suspended after assisting 66 developing countries. While the rich world is rapidly immunising its citizens, middle-income nations are struggling to keep up, and less developed countries must wait at least two to three years to even begin their modest vaccination campaigns.

Because of their inward-looking views, the developed world was unable to comply with the COVAX proposal, and the World Health Organization was rendered useless from the outset of the pandemic. The WHO has been distorted and swamped by great power politics, from failing to undertake an unbiased investigation into the origins of the COVID-19 virus to weakening regulatory requirements and granting emergency permission for Chinese vaccines. At a time when there may be more rising nations than at any other moment in history, the deterioration of international organisations will only serve to exacerbate world order disruptions and undercut the chances of a fatigued and weakened multilateralism.

References

- India's vaccine diplomacy: made in India, shared with the world, https://devpolicy.org/indias-vaccine-diplomacy-made-in-india-shared-with-the-world-20210329/, Mandakini D. Surie, March 29, 2021
- The International 'Politics' of COVID-19 Vaccines: How Did We Reach Here?, https://www.delhipolicygroup.org/publication/policy-briefs/the-international-politics-of-covid-19-vaccines-how-did-we-reach-here.html, Brig. Arun Sahgal (Retd.), Ph.D. , Ambuj Sahu, June 05, 2021
- COVID-19 VACCINE: THE JOURNEY FROM A GLOBAL NECESSITY TO A POLITICAL TOOL, https://www.firstpost.com/tech/science/covid-19-vaccine-the-journey-from-a-global-necessity-to-a-political-tool-9381311.html, MAR 05, 2021
- A Guide to Global COVID-19 Vaccine Efforts, https://www.cfr.org/backgrounder/guide-global-covid-19-vaccine-efforts, Claire Felter, December 27, 2021
- Vaccine Diplomacy: A New Frontier In International Relations, https://www.forbes.com/sites/saibala/2021/02/24/vaccine-diplomacy-a-new-frontier-in-international-relations/?sh=5137cd2b22bc, Feb 24, 2021
- The Political Economy of Covid-19 Vaccines, https://www.theindiaforum.in/article/political-economy-covid-19-vaccines, Jayati Ghosh, 05 MAR 2021
- https://www.indiaglobalbusiness.com/analyses/snap-analysis/smart-cities-indias-potent-weapon-in-the-battle-against-covid-19

Women, Vaccination and COVID-19 in India: Challenges & Issues

**Gurpinder Kumar

Abstract

The coronavirus situation has had a profound impact on people's lives and has continued to affect all parts of humanity since its inception. Despite such public health emergencies, past incidents have confirmed the general public fear and anxiety due to uncertainty, death, and lack of public health readiness. The second Covid-19 wave in India brought unprecedented losses. The poorest and most disadvantaged, including women and girls, face many risks beyond the means of attracting economic shocks and reducing health risks. They care for their families, furthering their livelihood and leading efforts to fight the corona virus situation, amid the threat of a third wave. More than 30 million people have been infected with coronavirus in India. Covid-19 can infect people of all genders and ages. Women in particular are the main victims of the coronavirus situation. Although women have lower levels of health and employment and face worse economic conditions, they also tend to have better immune systems than men, which could reduce the effect of Covid-19. Premature development of the COVID-19 vaccine is an important issue that should consider women's immune response to the virus and how to regulate hormones. Appropriate research has been conducted on vaccines targeted at women in the past, and women's issues were considered during those clinical trials to ensure that antibody problems and responses were correct and effective for women. However, some women and girls may be at greater risk because they are poorer and less experienced, or because they are at the forefront as caregivers and staff in the health and services sectors. The purpose of this article is to examine the impact that this unprecedented situation on the lives of individuals and communities has on its present magnitude. It will discuss issues of vaccination among women and suggest strategies for improving the health of the individual during the crisis.

Keywords: pandemic, health, women, vaccine, gender

Introduction

The pandemic Covid-19 has also exposed the importance of sex and gender in shaping the risk of infection, risk of disease and health information (Regitz: 2012). There is a significant interaction between sex and gender and other variables, such as age, race and ethnicity, and other health conditions that pose a different risk of COVID-19 exposure, diagnosis, illness, death and other consequences (Hankivsky: 2012). These standards need to be considered in the light of COVID-19 vaccines and vaccination programs. Gender and gender not only affect policy safety, efficiency and effectiveness, but gender equality can contribute to policy acceptance, access, access and, ultimately, the success of creating social security through vaccination and eradicating the coronavirus situation (Klein; Jedlicka & Pekosz: 2010). Global, national and industrial policy decision-making processes are also gender-neutral. Gender size is often overlooked, and female leadership needs to be better represented in scientific processes and policymaking. In India, women make up the majority of all health workers and more than 80 percent of nurses and midwives. However, when it comes to the decision-making role in the health sector, they are less likely, and earn less than their male counterparts. Only 13 percent of Covid-19 national members are women. As women in India spend countless hours caring for children, the elderly and sick family members, masks and other protective equipment are often designed and limited by men; women may be at greater risk of becoming infected. Currently, there is also concern that fewer women are vaccinated than men in India - 17 percent more men than women have been partially or completely vaccinated, and according to national data, there are only two counties where most women take over the goal. Because women have limited access to the Internet or smart phones, they may not be able to sign up for vaccinations. Because of existing ancestral practices, women may find it difficult to go to the vaccination centers alone, and there may be a preference for male family members to be vaccinated first. There are also myths that vaccines endanger the fertility of women. Unvaccinated women are at greater risk of contracting the disease, especially after new strains (UN Women: 2021).

Covid effects on women

Wage inequality and the burden of unpaid care have pushed many women into employment and poverty. Women's income in India was about one fifth of men even before the coronavirus situation. Worldwide, and in India, many women lost their jobs during the COVID-19 era. A recent report by the Center for Sustainable Employment at Azim Premji University in India shows that during the first school closure in 2020, only 7 percent of men lost their jobs, compared to 47 percent of women who lost their jobs and never returned work at the end of the year. In the illegal sector, women are the most vulnerable. This year, between March and April 2021, Indian working women in the workplace accounted for 80 percent of job losses. Indian women also spend more time doing unpaid home-based work than men. On average, they spend 9.8 times more time than men on unpaid household chores and 4.5 hours a day caring for children, the elderly, and the sick. During the coronavirus situation, their share of unpaid care work has grown by about 30 percent. The socio-economic abuse of women and girls has long-term consequences, unless policies and actions are deliberately directed and invested in women. There is a risk that women's retirement will remain permanent, not only restoring the benefits of gender equality, but also the benefits of GDP. UN Women data also shows that more girls than boys were dropped out of school during the violence and 65 percent of the parents interviewed were reluctant to pursue girls' education and turned to child marriage to save costs. This could create an entire generation of young women without access to education and employment opportunities (UN Women: 2021).

Covid and violence against women

With the closure of COVID-19 shutting down women in the home and their abusers, the level of domestic violence has risen worldwide. In India, reports of domestic violence, child marriage, cyberbullying, and the trafficking of women and girls increased in the first few months of the corona virus situation. According to data from the National Commission on Women, India recorded a 2.5-fold increase in domestic violence between February and May 2020. Some women's organizations reported that in the first four stages of house closure, they received more reports of domestic violence than they had in ten years at the same time. Some have pointed out that many women have not been able to report violence, as they have little secrets and ways to get help. The Indian government has classified domestic violence as well as support services as "essential" - an important step in responding to COVID-19. During the first and second waves of the corona virus situation, 700 One-Stop-Crisis centers remained open in India, supporting more than 300,000 women who have been traumatized and in need of shelter, legal aid, and health care. The current draft anti-trafficking bill to be introduced soon in Parliament is another welcome step, as it is designed to increase fines for perpetrators and make reporting such crimes mandatory.

Women and vaccinations

India has completely vaccinated 6.2 percent of its population (from 19 July 2021) and 17 percent of its people have received at least one dose of COVID-19 vaccine. However, vaccination rates have been declining and are currently estimated at around 4 million doses daily. Leading health organizations around the world have confirmed that people who have recovered from COVID-19 can be re-infected. There is not enough data available to say how long the natural immune system acquired after survival of the disease will remain or be protected from something different. Therefore, those who have recovered from COVID-19 should still be vaccinated. Vaccination can also protect people from serious illnesses, including highly contagious strains. The inclusion of vaccine in pandemic considerations in the current corona virus situation control research, policy research and development are expected to be the most effective anti-coronavirus novel. Several studies have shown that flu vaccination is the most effective way to prevent influenza in the elderly, reduce the incidence of serious complications, and reduce hospitalization or death (Nichol: 2007). It has been shown that vaccination can reduce the rate of fever by 35 percent and all deaths by 50 percent. The use of vaccines can often reduce the cost of treatment, and flu vaccines can effectively reduce the cost of hospitalization. Studies show that patients receiving the flu vaccine can reduce their hospital bills. According to the flu vaccine affect in Taiwan, where the completion rate of vaccines is 80% (and after deducting the cost of vaccination, testing, administration, and subsidies), medical costs can be reduced by 1.935 billion yuan (Lee: 2001). Most Covid-19 deaths occur in the elderly, especially women, and the risk of death is higher in patients with high blood pressure, heart disease, and diabetes, such as the flu virus.

Currently, most flu vaccines in the world are recommended for those over 65 years of age (Mueller: 2020), and in 1998, Taiwan began prioritizing flu vaccines for those over 65 years of age. As most countries cannot control the flu, coronavirus situation, the vaccine will be the weapon of choice for the elderly. In a global vaccination competition, the key to success or failure lies in the rapid production of vaccines and antibodies in humans without side effects (Arora: 2020).

Covid and pregnancy

There is no evidence yet about the COVID-19 vaccine that causes serious side effects in women who are menstruating, pregnant or breastfeeding. There is also no evidence that COVID-19 vaccines cause reproductive problems. In fact, there is a greater risk of severe COVID-19 symptoms if contracted during pregnancy. The WHO has also confirmed that breastfeeding women can safely take the vaccine and transmission of the active virus that causes COVID-19 infections with breast milk has not yet been identified. There is evidence that vaccination of breastfeeding mothers provides some protection for babies as anti-body fluids are passed from mother to baby.

The gender gap in India has always been skewed, as most health indicators, literacy rates and employment figures favor men. As India embarks on its massive Covid-19 vaccination campaign, the gap is widening and needs to be addressed. According to data from the CoWin dashboard, as of August 19, 2021, about 57 crore vaccines have been given, in addition to the total number of countries. Yet women make up only about 46 percent of the total population vaccinated in India. As a public health professional, I have seen this difference before. During my time with the Immunization Technology Support Unit (ITSU) in the Government of India, I visited several provinces to review, research and evaluate programs related to the Global Immunization Program. Respected as the world's largest vaccine program, it reaches 2.6 billion children and 3 million pregnant women a year with life-saving vaccines. In 2015, I founded the non-governmental organization Samarpann to address socio-economic problems at the grassroots level. Since the Covid-19 strike, we have been working to raise awareness of women and to achieve vaccination. In this work, I have spoken to many women - mothers, caregivers and leading staff in urban and rural areas. What I have found is that women's health is often overlooked for a number of reasons and that these challenges are exacerbated by the corona virus situation.

Challenges with covid vaccination

In early 2021, India launched the world's largest covid-19 vaccine campaign in all 3006 vaccination centers in the country. During the first phase, the program was to vaccinate 300 million people in all cities and rural areas. However, the biggest challenge right now lies in the implementation of the goal for most people, which is a very difficult task to accomplish. India's immunization program includes childhood immunizations and has a reputation for running the world's most effective immunization program, addressing the needs of more than 26 million newborns and 29 million pregnant women (NHM). However, the adult immunization drive of this level is completely new. Achieving this goal involves enormous challenges, especially in reaching people in remote areas. The team deployed in the immunization program should vaccinate approximately 1.4 billion people spread across cities, districts and districts. Managing an average of 3.4 million vaccines per day nationwide with 28 regions and eight union areas presents new challenges. During the first phase, the National Covid-19 Vaccine-Prepared Vaccine Management Specialist Team with key staff; in the second phase, this has been extended to include people over the age of 60 and those between the ages of 45-59 who have a related illness (Sharma: 2021). With the government's launch of the covid-19 registry website, participation has increased. Since March 2021, the government has also allowed the private sector to participate in its immunization campaign to speed up the process. However, the total immunization (both doses) has so far reached only 61 % of the population (Ministry of Health and Family Welfare). Although both vaccines used in India are now approved, an adverse event following a vaccination team was set up to address any post-vaccination problems. Without this program, skepticism about the vaccine still undermines full participation. According to the World Health Organization, the three main reasons for policy doubts are a lack of confidence (in the vaccine itself or in the health care system), dissatisfaction, and difficulty in achieving the vaccine (applications) (WHO: 2014). Some of these concerns are understandable, given the fact that both covid-19 vaccines were approved under emergency authorization without completing a full phase 3 trial. In a socially diverse, linguistic, religious, and cultural world like India, reasons for skepticism do not always lie in health matters, but are deeply rooted in the health and well-being of its citizens. Allegations of animal products, such as gelatin, in vaccines may contribute to law enforcement as they may conflict with the beliefs of some communities. India's biggest challenge is to mobilize people to get vaccinated (Aggarwal: 2020). At the moment, it seems that challenges with "well-known" (covid cases, hospitalization, and operational management) are being addressed, and India is going beyond "known anonymity" (managing vaccines and unexpected problems). The real test is focused on addressing the "unknown unknown" (short-term and long-term policy implementation, corona virus situation control, and economic development and health care). In India, unprecedented challenges of this nature are nothing new. With the emergence of new strains of SARS-CoV-2, India is facing a second covid wave. This makes it compulsory to vaccinate its citizens immediately to prevent further disaster. India currently faces the challenge of rising covid-19 cases, as well as the high number of hospitalizations and administration of vaccines. Further assessments will be found in the implementation of short-term and long-term policy, long-term capacity to control the corona virus situation, and economic recovery and health care. While uncertainty remains a way to tackle new viruses, giving hope to people is as important as injecting the vaccine itself.

Solution

All problems affect women and girls differently than men, due to existing gender norms and inequalities. In order to rebuild better and more equitably from the COVID-19 crisis, policy, investment and action must be shaped by women and girls and deliberately targeted. Make a donation to help women in India affected by COVID-19 UN Women works with governments and grassroots organizations to provide food, shelter, and financial assistance. Through our communication campaigns, we ensure that women have access to proven information about disease prevention and vaccination, as well as public awareness of gender-based violence. Through our programs, we make vocational education and training available to women through digital and distance learning, and help them find employment and small businesses. We are working with our international partners to provide shelter, financial and legal assistance and medical assistance for survivors of gender-based violence in COVID safe areas. UN Women also encourages government and private sector partners to invest in the legal and informal care economy to create sustainable jobs and increase women's empowerment and income.**Conclusion**

During the spread of COVID-19, women have experienced more stress and physical strain than men, and have suffered more from the threat of infection. Although women face worse health and work conditions and have a negative economic impact than men, women often have a better immune response to vaccines, which can help women reduce the effects of COVID-19 on them over time. Using information about better immune responses and hormone control in women could help researchers develop a vaccine for the COVID-19 vaccine soon, which is an important anti-corona virus situation activity. In the future, research and development of vaccines should also look at women's problems during clinical trials to ensure that antibody problems and responses in women are positive and effective. National policies should also put in place better strategies for female vaccination in addition to having a positive attitude. This will provide women with better vaccination information, which can improve their determination to get vaccinated in the future.

References

- Aggarwal, Arshi. (2020). *Faith or safety? Covid vaccines spark religious concerns over pork gelatin, cow blood.* Retrieved on January 20, 2022 from https://www.indiatoday.in/coronavirus-outbreak/vaccine-updates/story/religious-hurdle-for-covid-19-vaccines-religious-leaders-raise-concern-over-pork-gelatin-cow-blood-in-vaccines-1753992-2020-12-28
- Arora NK, Das MK. (2020). COVID-19 vaccine development and the way forward. *Indian Journal of Public Health.* 64(Suppl):108-11
- Assaf AM, Hammad EA, Haddadin RN. (2016) Influenza vaccination coverage rates, knowledge, attitudes, and beliefs in Jordan: a comprehensive study. *Viral Immunol.* 29(9), 516-25.
- Hankivsky O. (2012). Women's health, men's health, and gender and health: Implications of intersectionality. *Soc. Sci. Med.* 74(11), 1712–20
- Klein SL, Jedlicka A, Pekosz A. (2010). The Xs and Y of immune responses to viral vaccines. *Lancet Infect. Dis.* 10(5), 338–49
- Klein SL, Dhakal S, Ursin RL, Deshpande S, Sandberg K, Mauvais-Jarvis F. (2020). Biological sex impacts COVID-19 outcomes. *PLOS Pathog.* 16(6)
- Lee CW. (2001). The effectiveness of influenza vaccination of the elderly lived in non-institutionalized in Taiwan. Master Dissertation. Taipei: Institute of Public Health, National Yang-Ming University.
- Ministry of Health and Family Welfare (2022). Retrieved on January 20, 2022 from https://dashboard.cowin.gov.in/
- Mueller AL, McNamara MS, Sinclair DA. (2020). Why does COVID-19 disproportionately affect older people? *Aging (NY)* 12(10), 9959-81

- National Health Mission, Retrieved on January 20, 2022 from https://nhm.gov.in/ index1.php?lang=1&level=2&sublinkid=824&lid=220
- Nichol KL, Nordin JD, Nelson DB, Mullooly JP, Hak E. (2007). Effectiveness of influenza vaccine in the community-dwelling elderly. *The New England journal of medicine.* 357(14), 1373-1381
- Regitz-Zagrosek V. (2012). Sex and gender differences in health: Science & Society Series on Sex and Science. *EMBO Rep.* 13(7), 596–603
- Sharma, Neetu Chandra. (2021). *India opens vaccination for all above 45 yrs of age irrespective of comorbidity.* Retrieved on January 20, 2022 from https://www.livemint.com/news/india/india-opens-vaccination-for-all-above-45-yrs-of-age-irrespective-of-comorbidity-11616514379667.html
- Simonsen L, Reichert TA, Viboud C, Blackwelder WC, Taylor RJ, Miller MA. (2005). Impact of influenza vaccination on seasonal mortality in the US elderly population. *Arch Intern Med.* 165(3), 265-72.
- WHO (2014). *Report Of The Sage Working Group On Vaccine Hesitancy.* Retrieved on January 20, 2022 from https://www.who.int/ immunization/sage/meetings/2014/october/ 1_Report_WORKING_GROUP_vaccine_hesitancy_final.pdf

CHAPTER ELEVEN

The Cursed COVID-19 and its Consequences: A Critical Study

**Dr. Ratan Chandra Das

Abstract

The COVID-19 Pandemic has been causing a dramatic loss of human life throughout the entire world since 2020 and it has become an unprecedented challenge to the public health, food system, economy and education. A devastating disruption in the social sector, world economy and even in the education is caused by this unexpected curse for which million and millions of people are at risk of losing their livelihoods! Being jobless thousands of people are failing to find out the way of earnings and many of them are compelled to succumbs death as a consequence of the lockdown. The Business world is also affected very badly and the national GDP rate goes down to the lowest and due to its consequences, the trading system in rural area is also paralyzed. The continuous closing of Schools and colleges has stirred the entire education system. The teachers and the students are compelled to accept an alternative way which is called the digital platform to keep continue the teaching and learning even though its high expensive and beyond the capacity of the major section of learners who belongs the downtrodden society.

Keywords: Health, Food, Economy, Education, Digitalization.

Introduction

The sudden outbreak of COVID-19 has gradually been transformed into a pandemic and keeping its devastating mark on each and every sector of human life. At the cruel attack of this cursed disease, more than (55, 00000) Fifty five lakhs people have been deceased till date. (Coronavirus Death Toll and Trends – Worldometer, 2022) The paralyzed Communication and the destructive situation of the trading system have directly affected the public health and their nutrition. In the factories, industries and even in the agriculture too, the ratio of production is slowed down due to COVID-19. As a matter of course everywhere the number of employees is being reduced. Therefore, the poor are becoming poorer physically, economically and educationally.

The terrible affect of COVID-19 and its consequences

(A) The situation of averse to the society and humanity:

During the outbreak of COVID-19, the entire world witnessed how tragically has the human values and relationship been evolved. An atmosphere of uncertainty and helplessness is appeared in the society. On the way of home, the migrant lady worker gives birth of a child and dies of pain on the secluded road but nobody comes with a helping hand! Thousands take their last breath while walking along the path for going back to their homes. Yet none comes to help and rescue. It seems that the feelings of love, affection, emotion, tenderness, humanity, sociality, and responsibility everything is swept away from the core of heart of the people living in the society. Most of the people have become just like a machine which bears no reasons. Everybody fears to come in contact with the other as the COVID-19 is an infectious disease. There is no sign of humanity, sociality and responsibility. The fear of death is prevailing everywhere in this tragic period. This is the situation of adverse which makes man forget that man is for man sake and they are the social being who cannot live alone. (Bonetto et al., 2021)

(B) Disruption of psychological learning:

The pandemic COVID-19 has brought a dramatic change in the psychotic health. It is noticed not only in the adults but our students and the kids are also equally affected. Having been confined in a room continuously for more than two years, the learners are suffering from higher level of anxieties, depressions, substance abuse and disorder eating etc. The children are not getting any scope to share their problems and feelings with their friends. Their physical movements are fully stopped. Such type of circumstances generally leads to a hormonal disorder which causes harm to their psychological health. Therefore, the learners are getting failed to concentrate in their studies.

(C) Vaccination and its subsequent Consequences:

Very little is known yet about the COVID vaccine and the scientist are working day and night in that field to know how far it is beneficial. The crores of fund has been invested and the entire world is working together to find out a solution to get rid of the curse of COVID-19_! So, without any hesitation, one should get vaccinated at the advice and consent of his or her regular doctor. It is important for the safety and security under the present situation.

It is also seen that after vaccination, a large number of patients suffering from diabetes and leukemia are facing a problem of eyesight. Some are getting weakened and the immunity power is coming to an end. If these are the side effects of the vaccine, then definitely it should be taken before the attention of the administration.

(D) The impact on Health and Nutrition:

'Health is wealth', this great proverb is known to all. If physical exercise is a secret key for having a good health, then taking proper balanced nutritious food is another big reason to keep up the fitness. But, the present scenario of the whole world clearly shows that a critical financial crisis is going on all over the world. Under such a circumstances, when people are struggling for carbohydrate type of food, then thinking of nutritious food during this pandemic is a mere dream to them. The food system in human life is changed due to the new poverty caused by the pandemic COVID-19. The people find no alternative except negotiating with the quantity and quality of food. Thus Millions of men, women and children have become the victim of food and nutrition and most of them are now under the threat of death.

In a research it is seen that the people who are suffering from cancer, diabetes, kidney disease, asthma, heart disease, lung disease and also having pregnancy and weakened immunity system are at high risk of getting infected by corona virus and more serious COVID-19. (Who Is at High Risk for Severe Coronavirus Disease?, 2022) The study also shows that there is a higher chance of severe COVID-19 among the smokers. The people who have type two diabetes and blood sugar is not under control, can make an ideal atmosphere for COVID-19 to thrive in their blood. Beside these, COVID-19 may be the reason of death to someone who has chronic liver and problems in kidney. The study also notes that the patient suffering from asthma may be infected at any time and it may be very critical for his or her survival. So, it is very important to get vaccinated if someone has any one of the said diseases. But, the patient of heart diseases and pregnancies should consult with their concerned doctor before getting vaccinated.

(E) The Impact on Economy:

The pandemic COVID -19 is not an issue for the health crisis only but also a big threat to the world economy. It has already made a significant affect across the globe. Due to its immediate effect, the productivity is reduced, more than fifty five lakhs people have been died, thousands of business is closed, trading is disrupted, and the tourism industries are absolutely decimated. (Pak et al., 2020)

The COVID-19 has directly affected the global financial market heavily. When the number of positive cases started to increase globally, especially in the US, Spain, Iran, France, Germany, South Korea , the global financial and the oil markets declined significantly. In Europe and America, the stock market indices have lost a quarter of their value. Even in India too, the stock market indices got down abnormally which was a record in the last century.

The Indian economy also had to face the cruel attack of COVID-19 and even still now it's going on. Due to the imposition of lockdown and restriction, thousands of migrant workers suddenly lost their jobs and income. Factories, industries everything remained closed. The communication was paralyzed. The people started to walk to return to their home. Some died on their way. The people became distressed. The Government started to distribute ration at free of cost.

The Indian economy of \$2.9 trillion remains shuttered during the lockdown. It is really a devastating slow down in the Indian economy. The GDP gets shrank 7.3% in 2020-21. After the Indian independence, it is the worst performance of the Indian economy. The situation has yet not been taken under control but the Indian government and also the state government is trying to take the required measures. But yet, the Indian economy is struggling.

In every states of India, localized lockdown was imposed and due to that reason, the hospitality sector had to face a heavy loss in 2020. But in 2021, when the business was likely to be started, the second wave of the COVID-19 hit the nation and paralyzed the Indian economy.

After the first hit of COVID-19 in 2020, the people were trying to bounce back in tourism sector but unfortunately the second wave has crippled the entire sector. Millions of people who were engaged with the tourism became jobless. It's a tremendous blow to the Indian economy as it contributes nearly 7% of the Indian annual GDP. (Mangla, 2021)

(F)The impact on the farmers and Agriculture:

The Scenario of the farmers too has become deplorable. It is true that no restriction has been imposed in agricultural work. The farmers are ploughing and growing corn in the field freely. After ingathering the corns, he requires a good market for selling his corn. Thus, a farmer earns money. But, unfortunately a lot of restrictions have been imposed on the communication and trade. Due to this confinement measures the farmers are preventing from accessing markets, including for buying inputs and selling their products. Thus the domestic and international food supply chain is disrupted and the people's diets and food safety is being reduced. All these are happening due to COVID-19.

Still now in 2021, the COVID-19 restrictions are remained high. The working hours of the workers have been reduced. 8.8 percent of the global working hours are lost which is equivalent to 225 million of full-time jobs.

(G) Impact on Education:

Likewise the all other sectors, the education sector also has unprecedentedly been crumbled up. It is really very sad and beyond of our imagination how the schools, colleges and the universities are remained closed constantly for than two years due to the COVID-19. But the pandemic COVID-19 does not know to stop. Rather it's spreading out on its own way with new variants. Under such circumstances, it is really very difficult to predict when the cursed disease will disappear and the students like beautiful flowers will spread their fragrance in the classroom.

But its known to all that time and tide waits for none. So, the study must be continued. Therefore, a new platform has been brought up on the way of teaching and learning. It is called the digital class or online class which is the only one way before the students and teachers. It is a new horizon to the pupils. In this format the learners can customize the curriculum based on their speed and capacity. Here in this platform, the students can analyze what they require to learn. There are enough chances to enlarge their efficiency and productivity.

The online class is a time saving method where there is no need to travel for attending the classes and both the teachers and the students may have enough time at their hands to utilize. Here in this new platform, one can easily record the classes being delivered and he or she can go back that video again and rectify his or her mistake. Beside this, one can easily access various types of the learning materials. The submission of assignment, paper presentation, examination and even the evaluation all these are done very scientifically and smoothly through this online platform. Therefore, the importance of digital education or online classes can't be ignored.

In spite of the above mention facilities or benefit of the online classes, there is lot of difficulties or obstacles to run and continue the process of teaching and learning through online mode. The requirement of some electronic devices and the technical skill are crucial for running the online classes. But the major section of the students and even the teachers who generally do reside in a remote area especially in India, have no idea about the technical skill and how to operate the devices. To join the digital classes, the digital equipments or electronic devices are essential without which the digital class is useless. But, in reality, the major section of the Indian pupils does not have these devices. In a research it is noticed that only 8% `of homes `has managed to acquire these devices. A national sample survey report says that only 24% of Indian household have internet facility. (2020)

It's true that one can join the online classes from anywhere at any time. But when one attends the online class he or she needs to be attentive and properly audible. Otherwise he or she won't understand what is being discussed or analyzed. Therefore the learner requires such a secluded place where he or she can be attentive and clearly audible. In simple word, he or she needs a separate room which is a mere dream to those learners who do live in a single room with his or her family members. In a developing country like India, more than 37% of household have one dwelling room. So, these learners are being deprived from the blessings of the education due to the online classes.

The lack of electricity is another big challenge for learning through online mode. All the essential equipments are absolutely futile without electricity. But it's really a matter of strange that the most of the remote areas are running without electricity. The students residing in these remote areas have no chance at all to take the benefit of online classes. It is a great challenge for online classes. Those who reside in urban areas and have the financial capacity are enjoying the butter of the online classes.

Internet is one of the most important things for joining the online classes. But it's really very expensive. The learners of a major section of the society, who are economically weakened, cannot think of purchasing a data package of Rs.399. The services of internet are very poor in the most of the villages in India. During the classes many are getting disconnected due the poor internet service. Therefore, they have to wait for the internet to rejoin the classes and sometime they get failed. Thus the internet service becomes another big issue for the students of the remote areas.

The above discussion in this paper evidently shows that the digital classes or the online mode classes are useful to a minimum number of students who are associated with a family having the capacity to bear the cost of digital platform but not for the student of the downtrodden class. More than 1.6 billion learners across the world have been badly affected by the disruption of the new education system. Almost 24 million of students got dropped out who may not return again in the field of education. (Special Correspondent, 2020) Our digital platform or the online classes got failed to retain these students. But the schools, colleges and the universities are established to provide education among all the pupils irrespective of caste, religion, races, communities, poor or rich.

Conclusion:

The pandemic COVID-19 is changing its form and affecting the people with its new variant. So, the continuous lockdown may not be a remedy at all to get rid of from the cruel attack of the cursed disease. The business in shopping malls, restaurant in each and every sector should not be remained closed continuously for an uncertain period. Rather, the daily business in every sector should run maintaining the social distances and on rotational basis. And it's a pleasure to say that the government has already taken necessary initiatives in the matter to revive the trading and public life.

The Schools, Colleges, Universities also needs to be reopened. A teacher is the centre of the attraction to which all the pupils remains attentive to know and learn how a topic should be discussed or analyzed and how to extract the pleasure of the knowledge of the study. A teacher may not be knowledge giver but he or she can show practically in a classroom how to unlock the chain of the wisdom which is chained in the chain of black letters. But in the digital class it is not possible to do. This is why, teaching and learning on face to face mode is not a mere ancient system only but a great and the most scientific way of education. The online classes or the digital classes can never be an ideal platform among all the students irrespective of the poor and rich. The Online format is beneficial only for a little number of students who can afford the high cost and residing in an urban area only. So, thousands of pupils like beautiful flowers will be demolished in buds before getting bloomed out with the knowledge of education.

Reference:

- *Coronavirus death toll*. Worldometer. (n.d.). Retrieved January 20, 2022, from http://srv1.worldometers.info/coronavirus/coronavirus-death-toll/
- Lasalvia, A., Bonetto, C., Porru, S., Carta, A., Tardivo, S., Bovo, C., Ruggeri, M., & Amaddeo, F. (2020, December 17). *Psychological impact of covid-19 pandemic on healthcare workers in a highly burdened area of north-east italy: Epidemiology and Psychiatric Sciences*. Cambridge Core. Retrieved January 20, 2022, from https://www.cambridge.org/core/journals/epidemiology-and-psychiatric-
- sciences/article/psychological-impact-of-covid19-pandemic-on-healthcare-workers-in-a-highly-burdened-area-of-northeast-italy/ E112BA22EEFDD73599534AC313CA531F
- Hopkinsmedicine.org. 2022. *Who Is at High Risk for Severe Coronavirus Disease?*. [online] Available at: <https://www.hopkinsmedicine.org/health/conditions-and diseases/coronavirus/coronavirus-and-covid19-who-is-at-higher-risk> [Accessed 18 January 2022].
- Pak, A., Adegboye, O. A., Adekunle, A. I., Rahman, K. M., McBryde, E. S., & Eisen, D. P. (2020). Economic Consequences of the COVID-19 Outbreak: the Need for Epidemic Preparedness. *Frontiers in Public Health*, 8(241). https://doi.org/10.3389/fpubh.2020.00241
- Mangla, S. (2021, July 11). *Impact of Covid-19 on Indian economy*. Times of India Blog. https://timesofindia.indiatimes.com/readersblog/shreyansh-mangla/impact-of-covid-19-on-indian-economy-2-35042/
- (2020, July 25). Indian education can't go online – only 8% of homes with young members have computer with net link. CBGA India
- Correspondent, S. (2020, August 4). *24 million may drop out of school due to COVID-19 impact: U.N*. The Hindu. https://www.thehindu.com/news/international/covid-19-pandemic-created-largest-disruption-of-education-in-history-un/article32265660.ece

CHAPTER TWELVE

COVID-19 3rd WAVE

*Dr.Amit Kumar Verma,**Km Jagrati ,***Mrs Preeti Mishra*

Abstract

As the most recently discovered novel severe acute respiratory syndrome coronavirus 2 (SARS-CoV-2) variation of concern (VOC), Omicron's influence on our planet is rapidly growing. More mutations were discovered in this VOC (Delta version) than in the previous VOC (Delta variation), which may address Omicron's features. Omicron has been designated as a VOC due to these critical alterations and associated consequences, which include increased transmissibility, COVID-19 severity, and decreased efficacy of currently available diagnostics, vaccinations, and therapies. Notably, 15 of these mutations are found in the spike glycoprotein's receptor-binding domain, which could affect COVID-19's transmissibility, infectivity, neutralising antibody escape, and vaccination breakthrough instances.

Introduction

On the suggestion of WHO's Technical Advisory Group on Virus Evolution, WHO recognised the variety B.1.1.529 as a variant of concern, dubbed Omicron, on November 26, 2021. (TAG-VE). This conclusion was made based on data submitted to the TAG-VE that Omicron contains a number of alterations that could affect how it acts, such as how easy it spreads or the severity of the sickness it causes.**Omicron's current state of knowledge**

Many parts of Omicron are being studied by researchers in South Africa and around the world, and the findings will be shared as they become available.

Transmissibility:

It's unclear whether Omicron is more transmissible (easier to pass from person to person) than other variations, such as Delta. In areas of South Africa afflicted by this variation, the number of people testing positive has increased, but epidemiologic studies are planned to determine if this is due to Omicron or other factors.[1]

Symptoms:

In the early days, the symptoms of omicron include body aches, generalised weakness, weariness, headache, and fever, and later on, they may develop a dry cough, as well as a cold with watery nose, sneezing, and other symptoms." The cough is usually dry and goes away within a few days. Fever usually resolves within the first three days in 80 percent of patients, and if it does not, it is an indication of a mild to severe infection that requires constant monitoring.

The importance of isolating at the correct moment and avoiding infection from spreading to other family members cannot be overstated. That is why using the quick antigen is critical, and if the rapid antigen is negative but you are still experiencing symptoms, utilising the RTPCR will ensure that you do not miss any covid omicron cases and that you do not spread the disease to more individuals.

Even if you have to go out, make sure you're adequately disguised. When you have symptoms and need to go out for any reason, the doctor recommends wearing a N95 mask.

According to Dr. Harish Chafle, Senior Consultant In Pulmonology and Critical Care at Global Hospital in Parel, Mumbai, symptoms are divided into three categories: the most frequent, the less common, and the serious.

Omicron's most prevalent symptoms

Fever, cough, exhaustion, and a loss of taste or smell are among symptoms.

Omicron symptoms that are less common

Sore throat, headache, aches and pains, diarrhoea, a rash on the skin, discoloration of fingers or toes, and red or irritated eyes are just a few of the symptoms.

Omicron's severe symptoms

Breathing difficulties or shortness of breath, loss of speech or mobility, confusion, or chest pain are all possible symptoms.[2]

Omicron Variant Cases and Deaths in India and other country

The declining trend in new Coronavirus infections in the country continues. According to data released by the Union Health Ministry on

Tuesday, India reported 2,38,018 new Covid-19 cases in the last 24 hours, bringing the total number of Coronavirus infections in the country to 3,76,18,271, including 8,891 instances of the Omicron type. The number of active Covid-19 cases in the country has risen to 17,36,628, the highest in 230 days, according to the health ministry, while the death toll has risen to 4,86,761 with 310 new fatalities.

- Following a surge in Covid-19 cases, headed by the Omicron variety, India has seen a drop in new Coronavirus infections. On Monday, the worst-affected Delhi recorded 12,527 new cases, down from almost 6,000 on Sunday. COVID-19 instances in Mumbai fell below 6,000 for the first time; the city reported 5,956 new cases, down from 1,939 the day before. The number of new Covid-19 cases in Maharashtra has also dropped dramatically. On Monday, the approved 31,111 new Coronavirus infections, down 10,216 cases from the day before. The number of cases has been steadily decreasing across the country. According to a study by the Reserve Bank of India, Omicron could be more of a "flash flood than a wave." However, fewer testing on Sunday contributed to the decrease in daily cases. According to the health bulletin, Delhi only conducted 44,762 tests on Monday, the lowest number since November 29 when 43,499 tests were performed. The positivity rate, or the percentage of positive samples tested, climbed marginally to 27.99 percent. As a result, we can't draw any conclusions from the recent decrease in new Corona infections; it's still too early. The worst is yet to come.
- In Odisha, there were 11,086 Covid cases with a 15.62 percent positive rate: Odisha's Health Department recorded 11,086 new COVID-19 cases on Tuesday, up 597 from the previous day, and four more people died. According to a report, the daily test positivity rate increased to 15.62 percent from 14.96 percent in the last 24 hours, with 70,990 samples analysed. Bhubaneswar's district, Khurda, reported roughly a third of the new cases, with 3,469, followed by 1,416 in Sundargarh and 766 in Cuttack.
- The number of COVID-19 cases in Ladakh has increased to 23,536.
- Officials in Ladakh reported 152 new COVID-19 cases on Tuesday, bringing the total number of cases in the Union Territory to 23,536 and the number of active cases to 844. The biggest number of positive samples came from Leh district, with 132, and 20 cases from Kargil

district, according to officials. The COVID-19 death toll has remained steady at 222, with 164 deaths in Leh and 58 in Kargil, according to officials.

- COVID-19 deaths in Australia are at an all-time high, putting hospitals under strain: COVID-19 deaths reached a new high in Australia on Tuesday, and the country's second-largest state announced a hospital emergency to deal with rising hospitalisation and a manpower shortage caused by the coronavirus. The 74 deaths were spread throughout the country's three greatest populous states. New South Wales had 36, Victoria 22, and Queensland had 16. On Sept. 4, 2020, 59 coronavirus-related deaths set a new daily record. New South States' infection rate was rising, while Victoria's was nearing a plateau, according to Federal Health Minister Greg Hunt.

- On Monday, Italy reported 83,403 coronavirus infections, with 287 deaths: According to the health ministry, Italy reported 83,403 COVID-19-related cases on Monday, up from 149,512 the day before, with 287 deaths, up from 248 the day before. Since the epidemic began in February 2020, Italy has recorded 141,391 deaths due to COVID-19, the second worst toll in Europe after the United Kingdom and the ninth highest in the world. To date, the government has registered 8.79 million instances. COVID-19 patients in hospitals, excluding those in acute care, totaled 19,228 on Monday, up from 18,719 the day before. There were 122 new intensive care unit admissions, down from 128 on Sunday. The overall number of patients in intensive care grew to 1,717 from 1,691 previously. The health ministry said that 541,298 COVID-19 tests were performed in the previous day, compared to 927,846 the day before.

- There are 9,204 new Covid cases in Haryana, with 12 deaths: Haryana reported 9,204 new COVID-19 cases on Monday, bringing the total to 8,56,102, with 12 more fatalities bringing the total to 10,116. As per the health department's daily bulletin, the number of registered cases in the state has increased to 54,814, up from 51,253 the day before. The worst-affected district in the state, Gurgaon, reported 3,448 cases reported, followed with 1,435 in Faridabad, 799 in Sonipat, 649 in Panchkula, and 401 in Ambala. According to the bulletin, four people were killed in Karnal, two in Gurgaon and Yamunanagar, and one each in Faridabad, Ambala, Kurukshetra, and Fatehabad. COVID-19 has so far resulted in the recovery of 7,91,149 persons. According to the report, the state's recovery rate is 92.41 percent. Meanwhile, in Gurgaon, Chief Secretary

Sanjeev Kaushal met with administrative officers to discuss the Covid and the district's peace and order situation. According to an official release, Kaushal asked the district administration to keep a close eye on Covid instances and make sure that arrangements for oxygen, medicines, and other necessities are established ahead of time so that people are not inconvenienced. In Haryana, Gurgaon has the biggest number of Covid patients. According to the statement, Gurgaon deputy commissioner Yash Garg told the chief secretary that majority of the patients had moderate symptoms and recover under home isolation in four to five days. For Covid patients, roughly 6,000 beds are available in several Gurgaon hospitals, according to Garg. Only 152 sufferers are being treated at several hospitals right now, he said. He added that, based on the previous experience, the accessibility of oxygen in Gurgaon has also been boosted.[3]

Comparison in 3rd wave (omicron) and 2nd wave of corona[4][5][6]

Most persons who have been infected with coronavirus have had three significant symptoms in the last two years: a high temperature, a new, persistent cough, and a loss or change in their sense of smell or taste. However, the introduction of new mutant types caused a significant shift in it. Apart from these three common indicators, patients reported a variety of different COVID-19 symptoms, making it difficult to diagnose the infection at an early stage.

Assessments of the proportion of infected patients admitted to hospital in places like South Africa and the United Kingdom, where the Omicron wave hit first, provide some insight into Omicron's severity.

Individuals infected with Omicron between October and early December 2021 had a reduced risk of being admitted to hospital than those infected with other variations, according to a study led by researchers at South Africa's National Institute for Communicable Diseases - an 80 percent reduction in risk.

The analysis, that has not yet been participant, also compared the severity of disease once someone was taken to the hospital with Omicron to known Delta infections and found a 30% reduction in the probability of severe sequelae. However, due to the wide range of figures (confidence intervals) surrounding that estimate, it's difficult to say for sure.

While this would be great news if true, one flaw in the study is that it only looked at persons who were exposed during October and December (when Omicron was the dominant strain) vs those who were infected earlier in the pandemic. People were less likely to develop immunity earlier in the pandemic, either by infection or vaccination, although those affected between October and December may have already been exposed to another type of SARS-CoV-2 and thus gained some immunity, or they were likely vaccinated.

This could give the impression that Omicron infections produce less severe disease, but in reality, existing immunity may lead to a milder infection. Although the researchers took into account earlier SARS-CoV-2 infection and vaccination status, the chance of many re-infections going undetected remains.

- **Lung Invasion Is Reduced**

Another method for determining the severity of Omicron-related sickness is to infect laboratory animals with it and observe how they respond. This eliminates the chance of pre-existing immunity altering disease severity – but because mice and hamsters are biologically distinct from humans, it's hard to evaluate their reactions to the various SARS-CoV-2 variations directly.

This has now been done in a number of labs throughout the globe, and the results all point to Omicron causing less severe sickness than previous variations. These investigations also offer a possible explanation for the disease's lower severity.

Other investigations have found that the Omicron variant replicates more slowly in human lung tissue than prior variants, but considerably more swiftly in upper airway tissue. If this is correct, it means that the virus mostly affects tissue in the upper airways rather than the lungs, reducing the risk of pneumonia — a condition in which the air sacs fill with fluid and make breathing difficult.

COVID-19 causes severe disease through a variety of mechanisms, and additional research is needed to understand how the immune system reacts to this novel version.

- **An Increase In Infectiousness**

Also, just though Omicron causes less severe disease in people who contract it doesn't mean it's any less harmful. Omicron appears to be more contagious than the already highly transmissible Delta form, as evidenced by significant rises in cases in a number of nations.

If the number of community infections is allowed to rise, even a small proportion of patients needing hospital care can quickly turn into a significant number. This places a strain on already overburdened health systems, while the requirement to separate affected persons can lead to staffing shortages in critical sectors such as hospitals, schools, and transportation.

Minimizing infection and boosting immunisation access are the greatest ways to keep everyone healthy while also lowering the danger of new variations arising in the future.

• Mortality Rate

The third wave differed from the second in that it strengthened social distancing strategies later (3 vs. 15 days), lasted longer (36 vs. >56 days), and had a higher case fatality rate (0.91 percent vs. 1.26 percent). Between the second and third waves, there were substantial variations in transmission chains (P 0.01). The proportion of local clusters (24.8 percent vs. 45.7 percent) was lower in the third wave than in the second wave, while personal contact transmission (38.5 percent vs. 25.9%) and unknown transmission routes (23.5 percent vs. 20.8 percent) were greater.

• Covid Cases

With the third wave of Covid-19, powered by Omicron, sweeping India's largest cities, efforts are underway to quantify its extent and impact.

Based on statistics from South Africa, a mathematical model developed by scientists at the Indian Institute of Science and the Indian Statistical Institute forecasts three daily-case counts scenarios: 3 lakh, 6 lakh, and 10 lakh, depending on assumptions.

The Tata Institute of Fundamental Research has developed the only model that travels into this zone for the city of Mumbai. Hospitalizations are expected to be 50-70 percent of what they were in the second wave, while mortality will be 30-50 percent. Since over 4,000 people died in Mumbai during the second wave from March to June, the current wave is expected to kill 1,200-2,000 people.

In Mumbai, where the number of cases has increased 33-fold in two weeks, 12 percent of hospital beds are already taken. Despite the fact that hospital occupancy in Delhi is currently low, the state government has urged private hospitals to set aside 40% of their beds for Covid care in the event that demand increases.

Furthermore, due to Omicron's great virulence, doctors and medical personnel are at a higher risk of infection. In Bihar and West Bengal, where hundreds of doctors have been infected, staffing shortages are already looming. A fourth of the resident doctors in a prominent public hospital in Mumbai are unable to report to work due to infection.

- **Transmissibility**

On November 24, the Omicron variety was initially discovered in South Africa's Gauteng area. Covid-19 case numbers in the country eclipsed previous records within two weeks, with the variant spreading to 60 countries — a testament to its astoundingly high transmissibility.

Those referred to hospitals with Covid-19 were 73 percent less likely to have serious disease during the Omicron-led wave in November-December 2021, compared to the Delta wave in May 2021, according to one study in Gauteng.

The study also found that during the Omicron-led wave, only 4.9 percent of Covid-positive persons in Gauteng needed to be hospitalised, compared to 13.7 percent during the Delta-led wave. However, because the Omicron wave was bigger in magnitude, it resulted in 6,510 patients being admitted to hospitals, compared to 4,574 in the Delta wave.

In India, officials appear to be most concerned about Omicron's increased transmissibility, which could result in a significantly bigger caseload in a lot shorter time than the second wave. Health officials are concerned that this may overburden hospitals, particularly in areas with few healthcare resources.

Conclusion

There is mounting evidence that the novel omicron coronavirus variation is capable of rapidly spreading in populations immune to existing coronavirus variants. It has already infected many countries and appears to be on its way to infecting the entire world. The fundamental question is whether omicron causes greater or less severe disease and death. Researchers in South Africa discovered that omicron has a substantially higher chance of reinfection. This means that the risk of infecting vaccinated people is substantially higher than it is with delta.

Reference

- https://www.who.int/news/item/28-11-2021-update-on-omicron
- https://www.livemint.com/science/health/omicron-symptoms-how-do-you-know-you-are-infected-with-the-virus-11641952025690.html
- https://www.financialexpress.com/lifestyle/health/coronavirus-india-live-news-covid-19-omicron-cases-in-india-live-count-coronavirus-lockdown-night-curfew-guidelines-and-restrictions-live-updates-delhi-cases-mumbai-cases-pm-modi/2407790/
- https://www.gavi.org/vaccineswork/omicron-really-less-severe-previous-coronavirus-variants
- https://scroll.in/article/1014328/india-faces-more-cases-faster-peak-fewer-deaths-in-the-third-wave-of-covid-19-projections-say
- Verma dr. Amit kr, Mishra mrs. Preeti, "the corona return 2nd wave published by lexicon international publisher, publisher no. 5355/ISBN/2020/P

This content is not for commercial use, this is only for educational use.

CHAPTER THIRTEEN

Post Pandemic Work-Life Balance Strategies An Empirical Study

*P. Horsley Solomon,**Dr. Alok Tiwari

ABSTRACT

Pandemic being a health hazard, in the post-pandemic has brought it has led to numerous repercussions. With subsequent lockdowns around the world, companies have to move to the remote working model in order to keep them running. The concept of work from home thus becomes popular in each and every feasible sector such as IT (Information technology), education, etc. As the working hours prolonged after shifting to remote mode the line between the home-life and work-life started getting blurry. It called for intervention and inspection of strategies as employees struggle to strike a balance between these two lives. This paper's comprehensive literature review focuses on the study of important topics connected to work-life balance and working remotely. The research examines many elements of the work-life balance, as well as the most severe repercussions of new types of labor developed as a result of the virus.

KEYWORDS: Pandemic, Lockdown, IT, Virus, Repercussions, COVID-19.

INTRODUCTION

The word pandemic itself is used to define a phenomenon of global magnitude and thus unwanted to articulate that the Covid-19 Outbreak has impacted each and every sphere of human life. The Pandemic pushed humans into an era similar to the Jurassic world where mankind used to protect themselves by staying inside caves. The human world was drastically put into homes as governments throughout the world announced lockdown to control the spread of viruses. A new culture was introduced in the world of corporates i.e., work from home. Companies are starting to move into the new mode of online working with meetings, work and all the tasks were done on different platforms of the web. Starting from the IT sector to spreading to all different sectors such as research, education, teaching, etc. As the pandemic prolonged both the government and the private companies were looking ways for methods and strategies to reduce the burden of people and provide them with relief. People in general were stressed both financially as well as mentally and the well-being of employees was a matter of concern as it was directly related to efficiency (Saura, et.al, 2022).

The outbreak of COVID-19 has resulted in a slew of unfavorable and dramatic changes in modern corporations' personnel demographics. The COVID-19 virus has evolved into more than a health and financial disaster; it seems to have become a humanitarian catastrophe, especially for those already burdened by fragility, inequality, conflict, and sociopolitical polarization. Respondents with impairments and those who are in risk areas, and those with responsibilities to care for elderly family members, underlined in their remarks the difficult conditions they confront as a result of a failed work-life balance and a lack of assistance. The task for human resource management is to find solutions to reduce the negative consequences of work during the crisis (Pai, et.al, 2021).

Literature Review

The concerns like as global competition, personal life, and a shrinking workforce are causing work-life balance issues. Companies should invest in and monitor these aspects in order to face the difficulties and advance in the global market. Caste system, gender disparity in the workplace, and extensive informal working sectors are all issues that Indians confront when it comes to work-life equilibrium. The author also highlighted some suggested rules and measures that firms could apply in order to boost job satisfaction. Employees have a favorable attitude toward work-life balance and are able to handle both their professional and personal life effortlessly, while the rest are unable to do that for a variety of reasons such as a lack of ambition or a lack of resources (Edwards, & Leigh, 2021).

Employees' well-being has been influenced by factors such as feeling threatened, loneliness, working from home, and insecurity. Managers that need to adapt management techniques to new situations have a big difficulty. In order to operate efficiently, it is also vital to ensure the well-being of employees. Work-life balance is an essential factor that has to be examined and more assistance systems developed. Working from home has resulted in a build-up of professional activities in personal spaces. The physical barrier between the working from the resting area has also been removed. The distinction between the job and the leisure location also became hazy. Time pressures also have altered as a result of the growth of working time at home. As a result, the work-life balance was thrown off, significantly impacting employees' mental health (Habib, 2021).

The confined lifestyle zones theory focuses on the lives in the private light in the work-life equation which is conflicting, although family-related prospect and duties are critical to the category of difficulty that influence outcomes divergence. And though one's private life was hampered by the pandemic, the relations face of the work-life equation become more demanding, elderly parents who had to deal with new demands such as organizing or supervising learning videos for children and managing constant care that had previously been provided by schools or daycare centers (Babapour, et.al, 2022).

Gender bias becomes more relevant as the work shifted from offices to homes. In general, female was burdened with both work as well as with the responsibility of taking care of their children and home. It put a significant amount of pressure on women as they all struggle to strike a balance between the two. The emphasis on infant guidance and protection in the home prompts the study of possibly differing dynamics between men and women. There is a multitude of causes to believe that the countervailing force theory will apply more to women (Laker, & Roulet, 2021). The domestic attachment structure allocates the main duty for home and family to women as an ideal type. The idea of "intense parental care," which also emphasizes women having primary attention to the family sphere and, more particularly, caregiving obligations connected with bringing up a child, is aligned with the domestic love concept. Men, on the other hand, have historically viewed paid employment as the core realm, with their commitment to the "good provider" position exercised in that sphere. Notwithstanding certain cultural improvements, conventional gendered approaches to child care appear to persist, especially in the face of employment limitations. One might anticipate working moms to priorities family-related responsibilities above occupations, especially during a period of increased daycare demands at home, based on this more conventional gendered viewpoint (Mitchell, 2021).

For many employees, societal upheavals during the COVID-19 outbreak reshaped the boundaries between work and nonwork. The investigation of work-home integration as another potential moderator of the countervailing force theory is prompted by this reconfiguring work-home barrier. Even during outbreak, we believe that strong work-home integration will strengthen the opposing influence of children at home (Rajagopal, et.al, 2021).

The justification for all of this viewpoint stems from the description of the employment barrier as a gradient of total segmentation to complete integration under frontier & boundaries explanations. Job gets completed away from the home at a single position when fragmentation is significant; temporal and spatial boundaries represent the hostname's distinctness, with arrangements more akin to the "separate spheres" depiction of work and home roles as having different (often competing) expectations and responsibilities. In contrast, while there is a serious amount of work-home merging, there is minimal differentiation across responsibilities, particularly in terms of the location and time of work- and family-related role enactments (Imam, et.al, 2021).

Parenting and house management becomes a greater problem as employees are locked into their homes with no clear boundary of anything around it. Although the concept of work from home was conceptualized a long time ago it was put into practice during the pandemic. There is a lot of literature on how work from home is done both from employer and employees' perspective. There was hardly any research on how to manage the problems that arise with it. With no boundaries at home as to how work and life to be separated anymore, it added up to the stress of employees (Caligiuri, & De Cieri, 2021). Role-related problems were likely evident for parents striving to get their employment done without offices or venues outside the house to perform their work. Job and family responsibilities were pushed together, with many parents' spouses who were also striving to satisfy work obligations. Furthermore, work's intrusion into the family situation grew more significant as the house became the primary location for teaching children, and disregarding or neglecting children's demands on all aspects risked harming their maturity (Mello, & Grobmeier, 2021).

Parents may have considerable challenges in prioritizing job obligations over their children due to a lack of advice to augment the frequently casual and insufficient enlightening substance presented from school and instructor in the early stages of the pandemic's educational turmoil. Regular reminders that the extended parent role was really being ignored came with doing the task needed of them for compensation. When children were awake, these new and unexpected needs happened on a regular and visceral basis with so few barriers, even in families with plenty of space but when spouses occasionally took leadership. Every ignored inquiry over schooling, every demand for a nibble, and every moment a close relative had to set a miniature kid in front of the television or tape as a "babysitter" may have made parents feel like they were being negligent. Taken together, these characteristics appear to have aided in offsetting the general decline in work-life conflict proportions (Dajani, et. al, 2021).

Another important piece in our research is that the opposing pressure theories need not vary by age. The link between family at home and life & work disagreement, as well as how that relationship altered during the outbreak, did not distinguish both males and females. The relationship appears to contradict the premise that working parents suffered a disproportionately elevated point of life and work conflict amidst the outbreak. Keeping in mind evidence of who has shown gender disparities during the epidemic. The types of job strain encountered by professional women with kids in the early months of the deadly disease outbreak may not be reflected by the matter we are applying by means of quantifying it. In an economic meltdown of care, employment that does not produce considerable inter-role disagreement (as currently measured) might yet turn out to be necessary to fall. Working that seems to be close to the bottom, piece, but the less commended type of occupations which working-class women, especially less qualified, tend to just have kicked to the curb first when the teaching and care for children provided by different institutes went AWOL(Gigauri, 2020).

OBJECTIVES OF THE STUDY:

1. To analyze the post-pandemic work-life balance strategies
2. To ascertain the post-pandemic work-life balance strategies

RESEARCH METHODOLOGY:

The present study is descriptive in nature wherein the post pandemic work-life balance strategies was analyzed. The sample taken for the study is 150. The information was gathered with the assistance of an organized poll on a five-point scale and investigated with the assistance of the mean qualities and t-test.

Table1 Demographic profile of the respondents

Variables	Number of respondents	% age
Gender		
Males	73	49%
Females	77	51%
Total	150	100%
Profession		
Businessman	26	17%
Teacher	59	39%
Housewife	21	14%
Student	44	30%
Total	150	100%
Age		
20-35	52	34%
35-50	55	37%
50-65	43	29%
Total	150	100%

Demographic profile of the respondents

Table 1 presents the demographic profile of the respondents on the post pandemic work-life balance strategies. There are 49% males and 51% females in the study. Among the respondents 17% are into business, 39% are teachers, 14% are housewives and 30% are students. 34% of the respondents are 20-35 years of age, 37% are 35-50 years of age, and 29% are 50-65 years of age.

Table 2 Mean Value of the post pandemic work-life balance strategies

Sr. No.	Statements	Mean Score
1.	There have been massive repercussions post pandemic for every age group	4.10
2.	The work from home concept has diminished the line between work hours and family hours	4.12
3.	It is very important for corporates to consider and work on the issues related to work life balance of their employees	4.08
4.	In absence of a proper work life balance, productivity is hampered	4.13
5.	Work from home concept has had an adverse effect on the mental status of the employees	4.02
6.	Gender bias was another major concern that came to light during the pandemic	4.00
7.	The concept of work from home picked up momentum during the pandemic	4.18
8.	It is difficult to work from home while the kids are also at home	4.09
9.	Work from home concept is way more stressful for women as compared to men	4.07
10.	Employees who are able to maintain a proper work life balance, have better productivity	4.15

Mean Value of the post pandemic work-life balance strategies

Table 2 shows the opinions of the respondents. It is observed The concept of work from home picked up momentum during the pandemic is the most significant statement with a mean value of 4.18. It is followed by, Employees who are able to maintain a proper work life balance, have better productivity (4.15), In absence of a proper work life balance, productivity is hampered (4.13), and The work from home concept has diminished the line between work hours and family hours (4.12). There have been massive repercussions post-pandemic for every age group (4.10), It is difficult to work from home while the kids are also at home (4.09), It is very important for corporates to consider and work on the issues related to work life balance of their employees (4.08), Work from home concept is way more stressful for women as compared to men (4.07) and Work from home concept has had an adverse effect on the mental status of the employees (4.02) were also considered important. Reasons like Gender bias was another major concern that came to light during the pandemic (4.00) were also viewed as important.

Table 3. Factors affecting the post pandemic work-life balance strategies

Sr. No.	Statements	Mean Score	t-Value	Sig
1.	There have been massive repercussions post pandemic for every age group	4.10	7.478	0.000
2.	The work from home concept has diminished the line between work hours and family hours	4.12	7.776	0.000
3.	It is very important for corporates to consider and work on the issues related to work life balance of their employees	4.08	7.390	0.000
4.	In absence of a proper work life balance, productivity is hampered	4.13	7.865	0.000
5.	Work from home concept has had an adverse effect on the mental status of the employees	4.02	6.598	0.000
6.	Gender bias was another major concern that came to light during the pandemic	4.00	6.238	0.000
7.	The concept of work from home picked up momentum during the pandemic	4.18	8.564	0.000
8.	It is difficult to work from home while the kids are also at home	4.09	7.463	0.000
9.	Work from home concept is way more stressful for women as compared to men	4.07	7.123	0.000
10.	Employees who are able to maintain a proper work life balance, have better productivity	4.15	8.265	0.000

Factors affecting the post pandemic work-life balance strategies

Table 3 shows the results of the t-test. It is found from the table that the significance value for all the statements is below 0.05, hence all the statements regarding post pandemic work-life balance strategies are significant.

CONCLUSION

There has been a lot of research to suggest that work from home life is more stressful for women when compared to men. If one negates the struggle to find the balance between work and life, an increased level of satisfaction is been observed among the employees as it breaks the shackles of corporate structure. Employees now prefer remote working as it saves them from spending a lot of money and tiring commute. Corporations need to fund research to find better strategies for its employees to manage their lives in a new mode, making them productive. Considering analyzing the mentioned research areas inside the framework of the COVID-19 pandemic and the necessity to work remotely, it's important to think about which management strategies can help WLB improve when working from home (Liu, et. al, 2021).

A significant information source for both supervisors and people who work at home is recognizing the most critical factor of assisting employees to achieve WLB and sustaining psychological health when working abroad. Technology is critical in assisting WLB in working remotely situations. Technology can provide a stronger interaction among coworkers as well as improved monitoring of work by supervisors, according to empirical studies on remote working. Increasing WLB among home workers requires ensuring employee socialization via appropriate use of technology. This is especially important since research reveals that during the COVID-19 epidemic, employees feel depersonalized and disconnected. The development of employees' careers is an important subject of WLB study. The chance for workers' growth and training is one of the most important aspects affecting their good view of a business and motivation to report to work. a major impact of e-training on staffer achieving the best result all through COVID-19 (Ramani, 2021).

REFERENCES

- Saura, J. R., Ribeiro-Soriano, D., & Saldaña, P. Z. (2022). Exploring the challenges of remote work on Twitter users' sentiments: From digital technology development to a post-pandemic era. *Journal of Business Research, 142,* 242-254.
- Pai, S., Patil, V., Kamath, R., Mahendra, M., Singhal, D. K., & Bhat, V. (2021). Work-life balance amongst dental professionals during the COVID-19 pandemic—A structural equation modelling approach. *Plos one, 16*(8), e0256663.

- Habib, M. S. (2021). The need to redefine Work-Life Balance post COVID pandemic in Jordan.
- BabapourChafi, M., Hultberg, A., & Bozic Yams, N. (2022). Post-Pandemic Office Work: Perceived Challenges and Opportunities for a Sustainable Work Environment. *Sustainability, 14*(1), 294.
- Mitchell, A. (2021). Collaboration technology affordances from virtual collaboration in the time of COVID-19 and post-pandemic strategies. *Information Technology & People.*
- Imam, H., Afshan, G., & Samreen, F. (2021). The roles of negative career shocks and work-life balance in depression during pandemic. In *Academy of Management Proceedings* (Vol. 2021, No. 1, p. 12405). Briarcliff Manor, NY 10510: Academy of Management.
- Gigauri, I. (2020). Effects of Covid-19 on Human Resource Management from the Perspective of Digitalization and Work-life-balance. *International Journal of Innovative Technologies in Economy*, (4 (31)).
- Dajani, D., Zaki, M. A., Moustafa, D., & Adel, B. (2021). The Impact of COVID-19 Pandemic on Egyptian Women Psychological Empowerment and Work-Life Balance.
- Ramani, A. (2021). India's transforming post-pandemic workplace: The emerging role of the hybrid work model. *Corporate Real Estate Journal, 11*(2), 186-192.
- Liu, S., Ren, Y., Li, H., Liu, Y., Shan, J., Yang, L., ... & Chen, H. (2021). Prevention and control strategies for the post-pandemic era: finding a balance between COVID-19 and reviving medical service. *The Journal of Infection in Developing Countries, 15*(08), 1074-1079.
- Mello, B., &Grobmeier, C. (2021). Teaching Communication in a Pandemic and Post-Pandemic World. *Post-Pandemic Pedagogy: A Paradigm Shift*, 91.
- Edwards, M. S., & Leigh, J. S. (2021). What's the Plan? Some Ideas about JME's Strategy and Preparations for Post-Pandemic Teaching & Learning. *Journal of Management Education, 45*(4), 523-534.
- Laker, B., & Roulet, T. (2021). How organizations can promote employee wellness, now and post-pandemic. *MIT Sloan Management Review.*
- Rajagopal, K., Mahajan, V., & Ayyagari, K. C. (2021). Human resource management strategies of the Indian information technology sector post-pandemic. In *Handbook of Research on Sustaining SMEs and Entrepreneurial Innovation in the Post-COVID-19 Era* (pp. 191-210). IGI Global.

- Caligiuri, P., & De Cieri, H. (2021). Predictors of employees' preference for working from home post-pandemic. *Business and Economic Research*, *11*(2), 1-9.

CHAPTER FOURTEEN

Degeneration of Education: Impact of Covid-19 on Education

**Debabrata Nandi

Abstract

The outbreak of Covid-19 in India affected the lives of all sections of society irrespective of status, class, caste, gender and region. It had completely changed the lifestyle of every Indian. The Covid-19 impact was everywhere, i.e., in politics, in economy, in society and every aspect of national life. However, the impact of Covid-19 in two areas i.e., Economy and Education were catastrophic. In totality, it cut off the ongoing process of economic development. When it comes to education; this is also the biggest sector that has been adversely affected by this pandemic. The education sector faced Irreplaceable damage. The teaching learning and evaluation methodologies have been completely altered by this pandemic. The digitalisation of education became a necessity in order to provide seamless education. This paper identified the following as the overall impact of COVID-19 on education. Impact of it on the students of different age groups: time spent on online classes and self-study, medium used for learning, and the subsequent effects on social life and mental health.

Keywords

Covid-19, Education, School, Students, Online Education

Introduction:

In March 2020, a nationwide lockdown was imposed, forcing some schools and colleges to close and instructing students to abandon the usual classroom teaching style. As this virus spread very quickly from one man to another, therefore most governments have decided to temporarily close the schools to reduce the infection rates of Covid-19. Because the educational institution is a place where every day hundreds and thousands of students along with their teachers and support staff gather in its campus at a particular time. So, it was very risky for any government to continue school, college and university at the time of alarming increase rate of covid infection. However, later it was reopened in some parts of India where infection rates decrease but with the increase of the number in infection rates it closed again. In a developing country like India, the educational sector was tempered very badly by it. But at the same time, many new technique and way were emerged with the help of technology in education.

25 March 2020 was the last day when 320 million students attended school physically in India. Social distancing is the most essential preventive measure in curbing community transmission and flattening the curve and hence practical-physical schooling has, as a result, been shut. According to UNESCO, by the end of April 2020,186 countries have implemented nationwide closures, affecting about 73.8% of the total enrolled learners.

All schools, colleges and universities have created an online structure for day-to-day teaching and have also shifted online, postponed or cancelled many regular examinations, including entrance exams. This has increased the need for students to become adept at using gadgets and online platforms overnight. Schools where phones were not allowed now have classes entirely transacted online. Online learning has been observed as a possible alternative to conventional learning. Many educational institutions had taken the help of various technological innovations and continued their teaching-learning process in online mode. With the help of various online applications like Google Meet, Google Classroom, Google Calendar, Zoom and many others, many teachers started the process of teaching and learning which was suddenly stopped with the shutdown of schools and colleges. Many teachers were compelled to learn and many teachers willingly adopted the opportunity of these new techniques to make an effective class in online mode. With the help of Google Meet and Zoom, many students attended class, webinars and meeting from home with their audio and video. Google forms became a very familiar application. It was used rapidly in application, registration, examination. Google classroom became a mode for day-to-day activity between teacher and students. Teachers who are all experts in Blackboard, Chalk, books, and classroom teaching are really new to this digital teaching, but they are adopting the new methods and handling it like a pro to aid the students in the current position. However, those teachers who were not familiar with technological tools faced great difficulties in teaching and took longer to connect with students. The unpreparedness caused disturbed classroom sessions, interrupted lectures, technical errors and glitches and hence students took time to adjust to the new set-up as well. This required them to develop an extra skillset of technology usage and online learning. Various devices preferred by the respondents of a recent study for attending online classes were smartphones (57.98%), laptops (35.83%), tablets (4.89%) and desktops (0.65%). Mobile data pack was the source of Internet for 82% of the respondents. The majority of the respondents (62%) said that WhatsApp was the best way to communicate class updates.

To improve the e-learning experience, the education institutions are required to comply with the guidelines and recommendations by government agencies, while keeping students encouraged to continue learning remotely in this tough environment. Educated parents are supporting their children throughout the pandemic, but we require to understand that there are some illiterate parents and their feeling of helplessness to help their children in their education. According to ASER (Annual Status of Education Report), they have demonstrated with verifiable data that parents, even in rural areas, have shown full interest in their children's education despite the minimal resources available to them. As a result, this demonstrates a promising aspect of the educational system in terms of raising government awareness in order to meet their demands. On the plus side, with the increased use of webinars, conferences, and financial aid through volunteer organizations, things have improved over time.

However, the parents of the students were also in very stressful situation on the issue of fees hike in school. In many private schools in India, though no class was conducted but they changed fees from parents. In many private schools they issued fees hikes. In these economic conditions it was next to impossible for parents to satisfy all the demands of schools. This is why many parents submitted petitions on Supreme Court for a moratorium on the fees hike. Many provincial governments have already taken action against it. The High Court in Calcutta also issued a similar order.

Operating websites and appearing for class online has been a tough situation for many. Everyone has a different pace in adapting and many students are taking time getting used to screen life. This transition has also led to a variety of mental health concerns among students including signs of depression, PTSD, anxiety and stress. In extreme cases, students were also committed suicide. (2nd June 2020 in Kerala 9 students committed suicide because they unable to attend online lecture) Children are also disadvantaged by the lack of physical activity, sports and the exposure given by a social environment like the school. The balance in their lives has gone for a toss and consequent alone time has resulted in depression and even loneliness in some children. The mental health of students was also impacted by Covid-19. Students didn't just lose academic learning during the pandemic. Some lost family members; others had caregivers who lost their jobs and sources of income; and almost all experienced social isolation. The absence of school functions and social activity is being compensated by online group meetings and webinars and has recorded a decline in interest by students and teachers.

There is always a delay or cancellation of exams, which leads to confusion for many students and there is no room for curriculum. For instance, in West Bengal, two important examinations in 2020 the Secondary Examination and Higher Secondary Examination were postponed and a new kind of assessment process was introduced. Where the score of the previous examination became a yardstick of students' academic excellence. By which many outstanding students were deprived and many average students got privileged. At college and university level many examinations transformed in online mode with open books system. This open book system examination, though very effective in the western world, in India this made the idea of the examination just an academic obligation. Because in a country like India there was lack of proper infrastructure to take the examination in online mode.

Online education proved to be a great solution for short run but in long run, it created a digital divide. The shutting down of schools and the decision of shifting traditional classrooms to digital platforms is not only increasing learning inequality among children but also pushing a large number of children out of school due to this digital divide. Recent studies show that the students from less privileged backgrounds have experienced larger negative impacts due to the Covid-19 outbreak. Other than learning, the absence of schooling would also have a long-lasting effect on the health and nutrition of children. The role of the budget in the current situation as well as beyond the pandemic is very crucial to ensure inclusive education for all. For primary school students, online education is even not a short-term solution. Because for their overall development, social and emotional bond with teachers and students is very essential.

For a country like India, online schooling is a near-impossible step for 67% of the population that lives in rural areas and only half has access to the Internet. Availability of electricity is a significant challenge to taking advantage of education online. In a recent 2017-18 survey, the Ministry of Rural Development found that only 47% of Indian households receive more than 12 hours of electricity and more than 36% of schools in India operate without electricity. Some schools have even shut down due to insufficient funds and resources. The changes brought on by COVID-19 created an evident distinction between the rich and the poor and while the students who are privileged to have access to better facilities can still have the opportunity to avail of study material, online lectures and information, those belonging to harder luck are still struggling to achieve the bare minimum. In rural areas students have limited or no Internet access and numerous students may not be able to afford computers, laptop or smart mobile phones in their homes. If somehow, they managed to get a smartphone, they couldn't connect it with online internet connectivity. The price of data packages increased rapidly in this situation. Thus, Online schooling has created a digital split among students. The lockdown has led to extreme distress for students in India that come from economically deprived background. This indicates that those who have access to technology and gadgets performed better than those who could not arrange for the same. That shows that there was a big gap between the government policies for online education and its implementation at the grassroots level.

The Covid-19 pandemic has affected education in a number of ways, especially leading to the rise in the school dropout rate in India. Challenges such as gaps in learning and access to quality education existed for children from marginalized communities even before the pandemic. However, the digital divide and loss of learning continuity have further increased these gaps and decreased confidence in children. In a study by Child Fund India, 64% of the children expressed that they may drop out if not provided additional educational support. According to the UDISE report the dropout rate at the secondary school level in India is over 17%, while the dropout rate in upper-primary (VI to VIII) and primary level is 1.8% and 1.5% respectively. This report also confirmed that nearly 30% of the students don't transition from secondary to senior secondary level. The dropout rate among boys is quite high at the secondary level, as compared to the primary level. The main reason for dropout was their financial condition. Due to rapid economic crises, most of the school-going children are involved in child labour to support their families. This is also being referred to as a national crisis, with an increase in unemployment as a result.

Conclusion

Education is undeniably crucial in contributing to a country's welfare and an individual's growth, but it has been jeopardized by the emergence of Covid -19. However, most shockingthings was that there was a lack of proper bona fides of government to tackle this situation in the educational sector. Maintaining the covid protocol election commission of India as well as state elections commission conducted provincial or municipality election. Maintaining covid protocol market, Jim, cinema halls, shopping malls, bus, train remain opened. But unfortunately, all educational institutions were remained closed. To conclude, we can say that the Covid-19 outbreak has made a significant impact on education. But at the same time, it provides us with a new alternative i.e., online education in the educational sector. But to implement it effectively government and various stakeholders of education needed a proper line of action.

Reference:

- Choudhary, R. (April 16, 2020). COVID-19 Pandemic: Impact and strategies for education sector in India. https://government.economictimes.indiatimes.com/
- Jena, P. K. (June 18, 2020). Impact of COVID-19 on Higher Education in India. International Journal of Advance Education and Research, 77-81.
- K.Ramachandran, C. a. (April 14, 2020). Comment Higher Education post-COVID-19. *The Hindu.*
- Shafi, Z. (August 19, 2020). Impact of Covid-19 on Higher Education in India. *The Indian Express.*
- Rodricks Zita. (July 12, 2021) Covid-19 and its impact on education system. *Times of India.*https://timesofindia.indiatimes.com/readersblog/zita-janice/covid-19-and-its-impact-on-education-system-35076/
- Suresh Abinaya.(May 25, 2021) Impact of Covid-19 on school education in India. *Times of India.* https://timesofindia.indiatimes.com/readersblog/theenchantedpen/impact-of-covid-19-on-school-education-in-india-32475/

- Kundu Protiva and Shivani Sonawane.(2020) *Impact of COVID-19 on School Education in India: What are the Budgetary Implications? A Policy Brief,* New Delhi: Centre for Budget and Governance Accountability (CBGA), 2020.
- https://www.google.com/amp/s/www.actionaidindia.org/blog/impact-of-covid-19-on-school-education-in-india/
- Impact of COVID-19 on Education System in India. (n.d.). Retrieved January 9, 2021, https://www.latestlaws.com/articles/impact-of-covid-19-on-educationsystem-in-india/
- The Education System in India - GNU Project - Free Software Foundation. (n.d.). Retrieved January 9, 2021, https://www.gnu.org/education/edu-system-india.en.html
- Jena, P. K. (2020). Impact of Pandemic COVID-19 on Education in India. International Journal of Current Research (IJCR), 12(7), 12582–12586. https://papers.ssrn.com/abstract=3691506
- Rawal Mukesh. (January 5, 2021) An analysis of COVID-19 Impacts On Indian Education System, Educational Resurgence Journal. 2(5).
- http://www.education.ie/en/Schools-Colleges/Information/Information-CommunicationsTechnology-ICT-in-Schools/Digital-Strategy-for-Schools/Building-Towards-a-Learning-Society-ANational-Digital-Strategy-for-Schools-Consultative- Paper.pdf

CHAPTER FIFTEEN

Covid 19 Crisis: Present And Upcoming Challenges For India

**Jakir Ali Kazi

Abstract: India and the world are victims of COVID 19. India has crossed the second wave and reached the third wave. In this situation, we have to face various problems. Which includes economy, education, health, unemployment, poverty. Today we are far behind from the top position in the list of fast-developing countries. The question is whether we can get out of the covid-19 state but get out of this problem? This issue has become a big question for us today.

Keywords: covid-19, economy, unemployment, price hike, education, and medical system.

Introduction: For the past two years we have been going through a pandemic. At first we were only worried about covid-19 issues. Today our country is facing many problems. And we have to continue with these problems in the coming days. The next few problems include economic, social-political, educational, medical, unemployment, poverty, migrant workers, price hike of every necessary things, urban and rural income crisis, rising anti-social activities etc. But these problems are not permanent. We can get out of this problem. But the problem is that we have to keep a watchful eye so that we do not come out of these problems and face any new problems. So, we need a permanent solution. And not only the government but all of us have to work together to solve this problem. We can get out of this only when we understand these problems well. And I will take the right plan to solve these problems and proceed accordingly.

Objectives:

1.Learn about the effects of covid-19.

2. Know the current situation of covid-19.

3.Know the effects of covid-19 on the economy

4. Learn about the effects of covid-19 on education and medical systems

5. Awareness of its impact on the common people.

6.Knowing what challenges India will have to face.

<u>Present cenerio of COVID-19 variants :</u>

The current variant of corona virus is called Omicron. The Omicron variant was being assumed to be a mild variant. That's mean it is a less threatening variant as compared to the Delta variant. Delta variant was the variant because of which we witness the deadly second wave in India. Then it was an assumption of the scientists and experts l. But now several studies have been published by various research group in various countries that prove this is not a threatening variant. The first study was from the University of Edinburgh. Edinburgh is the capital of Scotland. They had used the national surveillance data to compare Omicron and Delta infection. The found that the risk of hospitalisation due to the Omicron variant was 65% lower than that the Delta variant. The chief medical advisor of the president of the USA said that the Omicron variant is almost unstoppable. Irrespective of how hard you try to stop, it would not be stopped. It will infect a lot of people and everyone will eventually be through this. Because it is so highly transmissible. Dr. Jaiprokash said the same thing. He is the chairperson of scientific advisory committee at the Indian council of medical research. And it was not a bad news because according to him, the majority of people wouldn't even know that they were inflected. It is being believed that 80% of people will get inflected but they will be unaware of it. B it will be so mild.

<u>Upcoming Challenges for India :</u> From the above discussion we can learn that Covid-19 can overcome a lot of health related fears. But the situation we have to face is as follows ...

Economic challenges : The economic crisis will begin as soon as the world gets rid of the Coronavirus. The whole world will start to slow down economically. Such a situation will start in India at the same time. India is heading for an economic emergency. An economic emergency may be declared in a few days. Such a situation came again in India in the '80s and

90's India was going through an economic crisis. In 1991, there was a plan to declare an economic emergency in India. But when Narshima Rao was the Prime Minister and Manmohan Singh was the Finance Minister, India managed the situation through economic liberalization and privatization. Although there are many differences between then India and present-day India. Even after that, looking at the current situation in India, it is understood that India's economic emergency will continue. At this time the government will have three options —

1. The government has to borrow from foreign country. India has already borrowed a lot from the IMF or the World Bank, so it will not be possible to borrow again. Borrowing from another state is not possible because every country will now suffer from economic problems.

2. The second is the introduction of a new currency. But it will be inflation. And without that, new notes are not possible in India in this situation. So the government cannot make this plan.

3. The third comes domestic help. But the problem is that the people of India do not have the money to help. Share market-crushing will not help large organizations. Ordinary and small traders will not be able to extend a helping hand. In such a situation, the only way left for the government is privatization. The government will be forced to sell bullets to the government. As a result, day by day we will move towards capitalism. Where 5% of the country's population has full economic power, capitalism will bring nightmares for the poor and the middle class.

Educational Challenges : India has been strengthening its educational system since 2009 – when the Right to Education Act (RTE) was passed, mandating free and compulsory education. However, this progress has been significantly hindered by the Covid-19 pandemic.

According to Observer Research Foundation, close to 250 million children in India were adversely affected due to school closures due to the early lockdowns imposed by the government in response to Covid-19. Several children from less-privileged circumstances ended up dropping out of schools, some were forced to take up jobs in order to support their families who were dealing with pandemic-related deaths and income loss. In August, Educational Minister Dharmendra Pradhan said that around 15 crore children are currently out of education system. The Unified District Information System for Education reported similar dropout numbers. The figure for dropouts at the secondary level was as high as 17%, and then there are children who have never been enrolled. These challenges amplified with the impact of temporary school closures due to Covid-19.Although private, urban schools in India were better adapted to new circumstances, government schools have struggled to transition from traditional in-person learning to an online ecosystem, especially in rural India.

Medical challenges : The covid-19 situation has shown the current state of the medical system in India. We have come to realize exactly what the shortcomings of India's medical system are. In the beginning our government and medical department did not give much importance. But when the number of covid-19 victims began to rise, the government opened its eyes. We all got to see the shortcomings of our medical system. Bed problems, ventilator problems, isolation problems, medical equipment problems, oxygen deficiency and many more. One by one all the problems started to come to our notice. But the good news is that everyone came forward to solve this problem in the highest way. Help was received from all departments. In particular, everyone comes forward to create an isolation centre. Our army, various NGOs, clubs and even celebrities and the Am-public all work together. But all of this is not our permanent solution. The question may also arise that we did not have to lose our loved ones because we did not work hard or because we did not receive medical care. There have been many reports of deaths due to lack of beds, non-hospitalization, lack of treatment, lack of oxygen.

So in the end the answer is that we have not yet come up with a solution in the medical system.

Unemployment challenges : During the lockdown in 2020, the highways of India witnessed the death of migrant workers. They had lost their jobs in Vine State and were trying to return home on foot. Last year, politics and movements across the country did not decrease. A recent report by CMIE, an advisory body to the Government of India, shows that the situation is almost the same in 2021. Millions are losing their jobs due to the second wave of corona and lockdown. There is little hope that they will be able to return to work soon. New lockdowns and curfews have been imposed in various Indian cities since last April. A survey conducted by the company in May found that the number of unemployed had exceeded double digits in percentage terms. In West Bengal alone it reached 19 percent. The latest survey was conducted on June 8. It has been seen that 13.72 percent of people have lost their jobs and become unemployed again. Most of them are from rural areas. In 2020, the number reached 20 percent. In all, about 130 million people lost their jobs. Eight percent of the people live on a single income. The report says that after the lockdown began to rise slowly in 2020, many people started getting new jobs. But if you look at the data from last February, that is, when there was no lockdown, the tendency to lose new jobs has been increasing. The reason given is that many small companies could not cope with the first lockdown. As a result, even though the office was opened after the lockdown, it could not be run for long.

Poverty problem : According to a study by the country's leading think tank, the centre for Monitoring the Indian Economy, 122 million people lost their jobs in India in the last month alone, most of them day labour small business workers. Economists also warn that the number of unemployed people will increase day by day - and not just in the cities, but also in India's rural economy. CMIE Chief Executive Officer (CEO) Mahesh Beas said, "The fact that 122 million people do not have jobs – a huge chunk of them, at least 91 million people do not have jobs today – if they do not have rice the next day. "Apart from this, Sanchari Roy Mukherjee, an economist at the University of North Bengal, says that the rural economy is also facing an inevitable crisis as millions of unorganized sector workers return to the villages.

Price hike problem: The middle class is now responsible for stopping the market in the city under house arrest. Due to the coronavirus, the hope of making a living on low savings has been strained this time. On the one hand, supply is low, demand is high, on the other hand, there has been a lockdown in the states. As a result, prices of essential commodities and vegetables have gone up a lot. Although the prices of onions, petrol, diesel, food oil and tomatoes were somewhat under control in early March, prices per kilogram have risen sharply since the lockdown, according to the Consumer Affairs Department. Under normal circumstances, if there is a problem in the supply of essential goods, the wholesale price goes down and the retail price goes up. But the wholesale price has also increased in the lockdown country. However, like economists and agronomists, wholesale prices have risen at the same rate as stockpiles have remained large and sales have fallen in some places. However, experts have blamed the shortage of supply behind the rise in vegetable prices. As the number of workers in these areas has decreased, the transportation system is not easy and as a result, the prices in retail have also increased. Meanwhile, along with vegetables, prices of edible oil have also gone up. Closed production as a result of factory closure. Which has a direct impact on prices.

Conclusion : According to a study by Oxfam, the world's richest people have doubled their wealth in a situation similar to that of ordinary working people. In fact, throughout the year 2021, the competition for wealth has been between Tesla chief Elon Musk and Jeff Bezos, one of the leaders of Amazon. This is not the end. In the last two years of Atimari, one millionaire has been created every day around the world.

India is no exception in the list Just as the bodies of migrant workers have been dumped on railways across the country, so too have Gautam Adani and Mukesh Ambani competed for the equivalent of wealth. The total wealth of the two has increased a lot. In the race to become the best industrialist in Asia, Adani has left the rest behind. In the same year, where thousands of workers lost their jobs in the lockdown and were forced to commit suicide - two of India's 'Business Tycoons' failed to make it into the top ten for a short time in the race to become the world's richest man. According to the World Bank, global economic growth is expected to shrink this year. Kaushik Basu, one of the World Bank's chief economists and a former economic adviser to the Indian government, says the country's economy has seen stagflation. The rate of economic growth is being limited to certain areas only. In such a situation, isn't the increase in wealth of the rich really pointing to a very discriminatory structure? Where wealth will be in the hands of one class and the other class will simply fall behind? What is the future of this world after Pandemic?

References:

- Dr. Prokash, Jay : "Everyone Will Get Omicron, Boosters Won't Stop It"(2022) https://ndtv.com
- The University of Edinburgh (2021) "Delta variant impact on hospitalisation revealed". https://ed.ac.uk
- Suresh, Abinaya(2021), " Impact of covid 19 on school education in India" http://outlook.com
- Vottosali, Amitav (2020), "Corona virus: It will be difficult for the economy of India to recover from the epidemic."BBCNews.
- Roy, Dipak Kumar (2020), " Impact of covid 19 on employment in India" https://timesofindia.com
- Mithiya, Debashis (2021), "treatment of economic desease"
- Oxfom (2022), "Ten richest men double their fortunes in pandemic while incomes of 99 percent of humanity fall". https://oxfom.org
- World Bank poverty Index 2021 https://worldbank.org

- Basu , Koushik (2021), "The Post-Pandemic Whiplash Awaiting the World's Poor" https://www.project-syndicate.org
- India today (2021),"How Covid-19 has forced the dropout rate to shoot up in India and what we can do". https://indiatoday.in

CHAPTER SIXTEEN

Inequalities and Discrimination around Covid-19 Outbreak

**Sk Abdul Khalid*

Introduction

In the wake of Covid-19 pandemic, nations around the world are facing unprecedented crisis with disrupted social, economic and political lives.[1] The COVID-19 virus, previously known as 2019-nCov, was first found in late December 2019 in Wuhan, Hubei Province, China,[2] before it rapidly spread across the entire country and then the world. Since scientists confirmed the possibility of person-to-person transmission, [3,4] massive orts have been undertaken to isolate confirmed and suspected cases from the public. In particular, as learned from previous experiences in controlling the spread of SARS, the lockdown approach was widely applied, and has now been proven for its effectiveness in controlling transmission. While these orts are designed to limit further infection, instances of and social exclusion have also increased as the number of reported confirmed cases continues to rise. This chapter is aimed to the observation and unexpected social outcomes of social inequalities and discrimination in the outbreak of COVID-19 across the world.

Globally Governments have step up to respond to several health systems issues which emerged with a growing tide of pandemic, however, very little attention has been given to the issue of sigma associated with Covid-19. Past experiences have shown that pandemics tend to provoke xenophobia, stigma, and discrimination. This was the case with Ebola and MERS, and

COVID-19 is no exception.[5]

According to World Health Organization (WHO), the current COVID-19 outbreak has provoked social stigma and discriminatory behaviours against people of certain ethnic backgrounds as well as anyone perceived to have been in contact with the virus. Several groups are experiencing stigma associated with Covid-19 including, people of Asian descent, people returning from travel, health care workers, people with the disease and their family and friends and people released from quarantine. Amongst all, people who tested positive for COVID-19, have recovered from being sick with COVID-19, or were released from COVID-19 quarantine are the most obvious victims. Individuals are being disrespected and discriminated because they are tested positive for Covid-19 and it is immoral just like any forms of racism, sexism, and ageism.[6]

Basically, confusion and uncertainty create a fertile breeding ground for stereotypes, bias, and discrimination. Humans as emotional beings have a well-established need to know the "why" of an occurrence, particularly uncommon and alarming happenstance. Why is the Covid-19 pandemic afflicting the world? It is important to understand that the stigma occurs when distance from the virus is confused with distance from the tainted person; when we shift the question from what is to blame to who is to blame. According to WHO, there are three main factors responsible for fueling stigma and discrimination amid Covid-19. These include: 1) it is a disease that's new and for which there are still many unknowns; 2) we are often afraid of the unknown, and 3) it is easy to associate that fear with 'others'.[7]

On the other hand, in this time of isolation, affected individuals have largely stayed in contact through social media and online apps, but the use of social media has also seen a rise in misinformation and fake news, which may negatively impact the health and lives of individuals, especially those seeking advice regarding sanitary conditions or treatments to halt or prevent COVID-19. Compounding the immediacy of the pandemic, patients infected by this virus may be receiving prioritized treatment at the expense of patients with other critical illnesses.[8] The strain on human resources, particularly healthcare workers, is acute when essential care and equipment becomes scarce, leading to competition between critical care and emergency cases, or even negligence of the elderly, those with special disabilities, as well as indigenous, homeless, migrant and imprisoned populations.[9] Border closure, limiting the international or transnational movement of individuals, or imposed travel restrictions, worsened the plight of asylum seekers and undocumented migrants. These travel restrictions might be a violation of International Health Regulations if the restriction infringes upon rights of movement to seek a better or viable health solution.

There was a rise in anti-Chinese sentiment, or racism, causing shame and stress to Chinese nationals or even to other Asians, and thus stigmatization. Such prejudice often arises with the need for self-protection, and the fear underlying this need for a racialized response to the COVID-19 threat led to some panic and hysteria, microaggressions and mass generalizations, even spates of violence and protests, causing the disproportional victimization of ethnic minorities and socio-economic discrimination of marginalized groups, made worse by erroneous misinformation.

Curtailed movement and choices, or intrusive and forcefully imposed policies, restrictions or regulations, the use of state surveillance, drones, forced implementation of mobile apps to track citizens and the spread of COVID-19, color coding for citizens based on their travel and health status, as well as profiling, even under the premise of protecting society's health, may be used to fortify state control and surveillance, possibly restricting civil liberties, or freedoms and rights, thereby raising privacy concerns by suspending democratic deliberation or fortifying authoritarianism. COVID-19 might fortify other psychosocial and structural burdens, including misogyny, homophobia, homelessness and mental health.

Experiences from previous epidemics and pandemics have shown that stigmatization of certain groups can drive people to hide their diagnosis to avoid discrimination, discourage them from seeking health care and prevent them from practicing healthy behaviors. Perhaps more concerning, stigma negatively influences the emotional, mental, and physical health of discriminated groups and the communities they live in. In the longer term, stigmatization and discrimination can undermine social inclusion and prompt possible social isolation of groups, which might contribute to a condition where the virus is more, not less, likely to spread.[10]

In this pandemic, and in post-COVID-19 societies, the challenges that humanity faces as a result of limitations need to be addressed now, prior to the arrival of the next pandemic, or the resurgence of this one. If the healthy versus sick dividing line can be better appreciated through solid science- and evidence-based medicine, and if proper public health governance and policies can be effectively implemented through resolute political leadership, then more compassion towards those infected by COVID-19, or respect towards others that are mistreated as a result of this pandemic, including those who recovered from COVID-19 and are living a post-infection life, may emerge and prevail.

To tackle this aspect of the crisis, health strategies should not only focus on the medical dimensions of the pandemic but also the human rights specific consequences of Covid-19. WHO endorses that as we collectively work to contain the Covid-19 spread; governments, citizens, media, key influencers and communities should also step up to counter the contagion of prejudice and stigma. To avoid fuelling fear and stigma around Covid-19, it is important to build trust in reliable health information sources, show empathy and maintain privacy and confidentiality of those affected, avoid use of negative language that can cause stigma, give people freedom to speak out against negative behaviours and statements, and amplify the voices of people with lived experience of coronavirus. More importantly, an enabling environment needs to be ensured in which Covid-19 and its impact can be discussed and addressed freely, ethically, and efficiently. It is significant to recognize the fact that Covid-19 is a common enemy that does not care about ethnicity or nationality, faction, or faith. "It attacks all, relentlessly." Thus, its high time that all individuals around the globe, should strengthen the immunity not only against Covid-19 but also against the 'virus of hate'.[11]

References

1. WHO Coronavirus Disease (COVID-19) Dashboard. World Health Organization. (2020b) Retrieved from https://covid19.who.int/.
2. Huang, C.; Wang, Y.; Li, X.; Ren, L.; Zhao, J.; Hu, Y.; Cheng, Z. Clinical features of patients infected with 2019 novel coronavirus in Wuhan, China. Lancet 2020, 395, 497–506.
3. Zhu, N.; Zhang, D.; Wang, W. A novel coronavirus from patients with pneumonia in China, 2019. N. Engl. J. Med. 2020.
4. Chan, J.F.-W.; Yuan, S.; Kok, K.-H. A familial cluster of pneumonia associated with the 2019 novel coronavirus indicating person-to-person transmission: A study of a family cluster. Lancet 2020, 395, 514–523.
5. American Psychological Association. (2020). Combating bias and stigma related to COVID-19. In.
6. Corrigan, Patrick.. On the Stigma of COVID-19. Let's separate the illness from the patient. (2020) Retrieved from

https://www.psychologytoday.com/us/blog/the-stigma-effect/ 202004/the-stigma-covid-19.

7. Social Stigma associated with COVID-19. A guide to preventing and addressing social stigma. UNICEF, WHO, IFRC (2020) https://www.epiwin. com/sites/epiwin/files/content/attachments/ 2020-02-24/COVID19% 20Stigma% 20Guide% 2024022020_1. pdf adresinden erişilmiştir.

8. Baker T, Schell CO, Petersen DB, et al. Essential care of critical illness must not be forgotten in the COVID-19 pandemic.

9. Vieira CM, Franco OH, Restrepo CG, Abel T. COVID-19: The forgotten priorities of the pandemic. Maturitas 2020; 136:38-41.

10. Corrigan, Patrick.. On the Stigma of COVID-19. Let's separate the illness from the patient. (2020) Retrieved from https://www.psychologytoday.com/us/blog/the-stigma-effect/ 202004/the-stigma-covid-19.

11. Stop the coronavirus stigma now. 580(7802), 165. Nature. (2020).

Covid Pandemic Crisis On Media & Entertainment Industry

*Ms. Nikita Jain, **Dr. Seema Nath Jain, ***Dr. Anshika Rajvanshi*

Introduction

The coronavirus pandemic is having a tremendous impact on sectors across India, including the music and entertainment industry. Public meetings have been outlawed, and theatres, theatres, music festivals, plays, and concerts have been shuttered or cancelled permanently as a result of the virus's deployment of lockdowns across all states. The Bollywood business was struck hard almost immediately, with movie theatres closing throughout the country and key blockbusters being postponed. Even once the lockdowns are removed, the demand for social separation may become the norm, with major consequences for those in the entertainment business who rely on the creation and distribution of music, movies, and related live events to make a living. The pandemic's effects on these sectors might include reduced attendance at film festivals and music concerts, delays in film distribution, delayed or cancelled movie releases, and a reduction in on-location filming. Production companies, music labels, filmmakers, artists, and theatre owners, among others, will most certainly suffer financial consequences for months, if not years. The following are the significant legal issues:

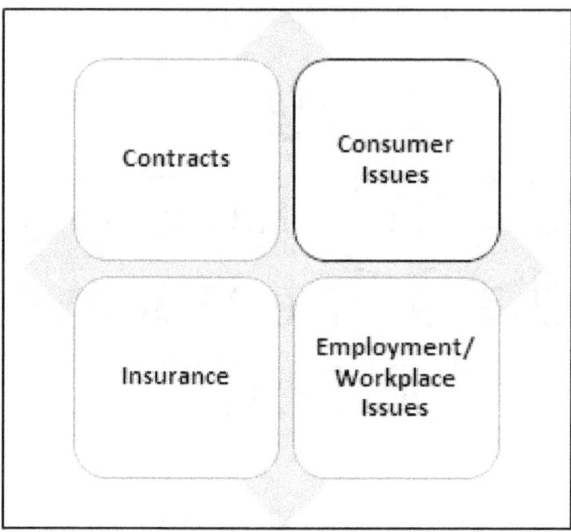

Figure 1 Major Legal Issues related to Media & Entertainment Industries

Agreements

Content owners, production houses, artists, investors, sponsors, promoters, distributors, vendors, production companies, broadcasters, ticketing agencies, theatres, and licensors are all part of the film industry.

The risk of non-performance, poor performance, delay, and non-payment is increased as a result of the disruptive impact of a worldwide pandemic leading in the shutdown of workforces, closing of borders, and forced work from home arrangements. Physical agreements are proving difficult to implement. Cancellation of film releases, premieres, and events raised a slew of practical issues, including potential refunds, exchanges, and contractual obligations, particularly for interested parties such as sponsors, broadcasters, and ticket holders who may have invested large sums of money and are now facing uncertainty and losses. Some contracts directly address these difficulties in their provisions, while in others, contractual concepts such as frustration will govern the parties' rights.

End Users Affairs

The cancellation of live events has given rise to potential consumer protection claims. Companies have found difficulties in refunding money to ticketholders, putting pressure on the industry's already sluggish economy.

In light of this, the Central Board of Indirect Taxes and Customs (CBIC) has permitted firms to seek refunds of Goods and Services Tax (GST) paid on advances for events or bookings that were later cancelled. The government's action is likely to benefit the entertainment business, since the increased cash will boost firms' liquidity positions, which can then be utilised to keep the economy in control and keep people employed.

Security

Business Interruption Coverage: Businesses must determine if their insurance plans will reimburse them for damages incurred as a result of the pandemic's lengthy stoppage of operations. The amount of insurance coverage available to a business is determined by the conditions of each policy.

While businesses purchase insurance to protect themselves from business disruption, such plans may not often cover pandemics like Covid-19. According to insurers, business interruption coverage kicks in only if the insured property sustains physical damage as a result of a covered risk like fire or earthquake, and it does not cover losses caused by a pandemic like COVID 19. Companies are now requesting that the Insurance Regulatory and Development Authority of India (IRDA) broaden the extent of its regulatory authority.

Working Environment Measures

The entertainment industry's workforce is mostly made up of casual workers or contractors who do not have access to paid time off and hence risk losing their jobs. Because production and distribution are almost at a halt, businesses will attempt to cut expenses sooner rather than later, resulting in salary cutbacks and layoffs for causes beyond the employer's control. However, these are challenging judgments that can have a significant impact on people's livelihoods, and they often need thorough evaluation of facts to ascertain the genuine nature of an employment connection.

Another critical problem at hand is the management of the workplace environment and guaranteeing the safety of its employees when they return to work. Over the years, workplace trends have changed. Prior to the pandemic, enclosed offices gave way to cubicles, which gave way to open ideas without walls, and social separation at work wasn't precisely the norm. Employees are more likely to report to work even if their health is impaired, which might transmit the infection further.

The Silver Lining

Even while the entertainment industry's future appears to be bleak, there appears to be a silver lining, with digital OTT platforms, music streaming services, and radio all witnessing continuous growth in their business models. As per a KPMG analysis, with individuals confined to their residences, the consumption of material on these platforms has experienced a boom both in terms of hours spent and new consumers. Due of the risk of getting the infectious illness, people have more likely turned to in-home entertainment alternatives such as digital, television, and gaming, which scientists predict will eventually lead to habit building.

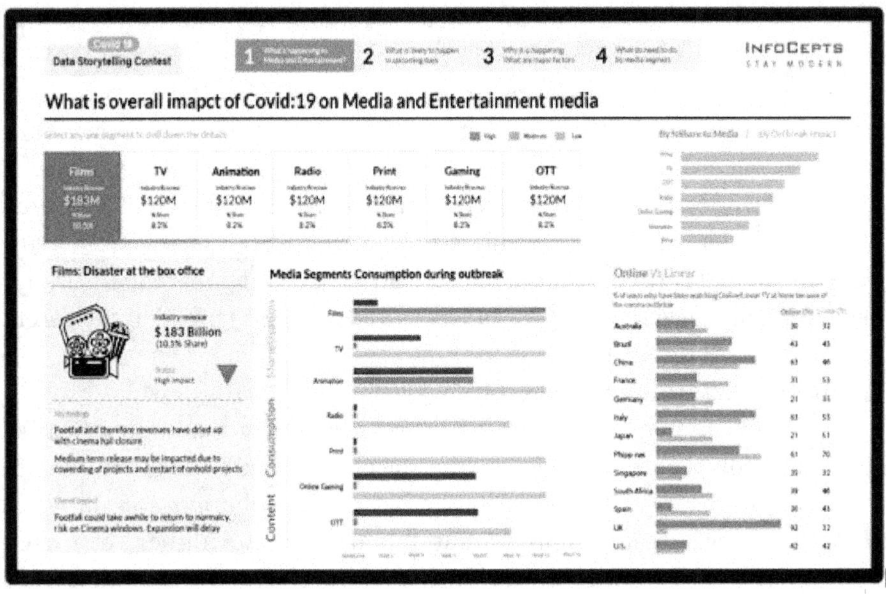

Figure 2 Overall Impact of Covid Pandemic: showing various platforms with their % of Industry revenue

Major studios are now considering digital releases of films on OTT platforms, as box office sales are expected to decline owing to the high possibility of consumers avoiding crowded places for a time.

Angrezi Medium, a film starring Irrfan Khan that underperformed at the box office due to a sudden announcement of tight lockdown across multiple states in 2019, was re-released on Hotstar in 2020 to appeal to consumers at home. "Gulaabo Sitaabo," starring Amitabh Bacchan and Ayushmaan Khurrana, also decided to forego its theatrical release in favour of a digital release on Amazon Prime Video, with many other major studios following suit. Aamir Khan, Alia Bhatt, Ranbir Kapoor, Vicky Kaushal, Bhumi Pednekar, and Deepika Padukone are among the Indian celebs who have tested positive in recent months and have had treatment.

While film shoots resumed and theatres gradually reopened in October 2021 with restricted seating, the destruction inflicted by the continuing second and third wave has thrown everything to a standstill. Due to the epidemic, the enormously famous cricket tournament Indian Premier League, which has been a huge streaming hit for Disney+ Hotstar, had to be halted in the middle of its season. Attempts to keep India's most popular game alive despite the current wave's carnage were greeted with significant criticism over the resources used to protect affluent and healthy players, pushing organisers to agree to a complete, long-term halt.

The Producers Guild of India president Siddharth Roy Kapur tells The Hollywood Reporter, "Everyone is making plans and contingencies based on an estimation of when things will open up, but there is no way of knowing." "It's like making plans on the beach, just to have them washed away by the waves before you realise it."

Following the installation of lockdowns in the western state of Maharashtra, home to the country's entertainment capital, Mumbai, practically every major Indian film production is on pause. While certain projects, mainly for television series with indoor sets, were temporarily relocated to other states, such as Goa, the intensity of the second and third wave has thrown everything to a halt across the country. Many large cities are also enforcing curfews and lockdowns, including the national capital Delhi, which is a favourite filming destination but is also the pandemic's worst-affected major population centre. Kapur, who formerly led the Walt Disney Company in India, now operates his own production company, Roy Kapur Films, which has had a number of projects halted. He claims that the interruption to the company's films and series is "mirrored all throughout the industry."

Similarly, Amazon Prime Video's debut Indian feature co-production, Ram Setu, starring superstar Akshay Kumar, is currently on hold. In last year April, Kumar tested positive and was briefly hospitalized but recovered soon after.

Meanwhile, as the country embarks on a large vaccination blitz — over 170 million shots have been provided so far — certain industrial business bodies are stepping in to help the government's lagging public health efforts.

Yash Raj Films, India's largest production company, have immunised over 30,000 members of the Federation of Western India Cine Employees. The business got access to these vaccines by requesting to Maharashtra Chief Minister Uddhav Thackeray permission to buy vaccinations. In addition, through the non-profit organisation Youth Feed India, YRF's Yash Chopra Foundation will launch a direct benefit transfer of $68 (5,000 rupees) to women and elderly citizens in the sector, as well as provide ration packages to employees for a month to a family of four.

IMPACT on Media & Entertainment Industry: WORLDWIDE

To maintain social distance conventions, Dubai provided a drive-in movie theatre on the roof of one of its malls for its moviegoers. To survive this epidemic, a new approach would be required. The globe appears to be listening into the radio, and digital radio's performance during the coronavirus pandemic reflects people's desire to keep informed. According to the BBC, its radio properties have seen an 18% growth in streaming. Consumers are turning to radio as a trusted source of knowledge and community connection at a time of increased uncertainty and interrupted habits.

With all of the festival cancellations and postponements – such as Glastonbury Festival in the United Kingdom, Coachella in the United States, and Burning Man in the United States – live concerts and tours, artists have had to come up with new ways to interact with their fans during the global downturn. Through social media networks such as Instagram, Twitter, and Facebook, musicians are organising their own concerts from the comfort of their studios.

The Walt Disney Company India and its Star network have pledged a $6.8 million contribution to local Covid-19 relief efforts, up from $3.8 million last year.

Daily wage employees engaged in different capacities in film and television teams have been impacted particularly hard as productions have paused. Last year, the Producers Guild established a worker assistance fund, to which Netflix contributed $1 million. The Guild is reaching out to its members again to seek donations. While the Guild has yet to announce data, it is expected that the relief fund has raised over $2 million between last year and this year.

Analysts predict that the financial effect of the epidemic have worsen the situation in 2021 than it was in 2020. According to an annual report by consultants Ernst and Young, total revenue for India's media and entertainment industry — which includes all sectors such as film, digital, TV, music, print, animation, and gaming, among others — fell by 24% in 2021 to $18.7 billion (1.38 trillion rupees) from $24.7 billion (1.82 trillion rupees) in 2020, "effectively returning revenues to 2017 levels."

OTT PLATFORMS and GAMING & ANIMATION INDUSTRIES

During the lockdown period, TV, gaming, digital and OTT platforms are seeing consumption growth. On the other hand, outdoor consumption models such as films, events, theme parks, are witnessing a dramatic fall with social distancing norms in place, news agency IANS reported.

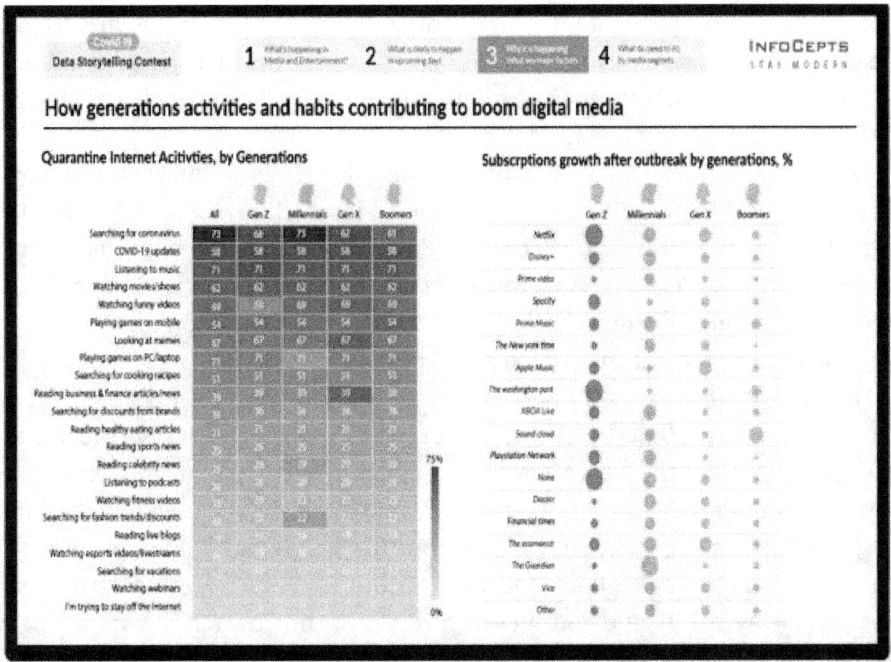

Figure 3 Share of various Digital Media on various OTT platforms

"During the shutdown, digital media consumption, notably OTT, has increased in terms of both time spent and new viewers. Once the situation around Covid-19 is under control, the resulting habit development is likely to result in a new higher normal "it was written. It also stated that "because to the lockdown effect with broadband internet," OTT consumption in India may begin to transfer from the smartphone screen to the huge TV screen.

Media businesses, particularly OTT platforms, may seriously consider gaming as an extension to their ecosystem services, gaming is another area that might gain from the whole digital ecosystem. It projected that sports might emerge as the main draw when recovery begins, especially when IPL dates are released. When it comes to movies, the study states that footfalls and hence income have dried up due to cinema hall closures. Overall, footfalls may take some time to recover to normal, with the danger of theatrical windows shortening and expansion delays.

OTTs do have a silver lining. Despite the fact that the content pipeline has dried up, the platforms now have a larger, more lively library, which is working to their advantage. It was pointed out that OTT players are giving lengthier free periods to encourage subscriptions through habit building. It suggests that habit-building might lead to a new normal and faster consumption and monetization growth.

Another industry that is expected to flourish is animation. Because animation and visual effects are more long-term, demand may be able to withstand the downturn. While television and internet projects are expected to grow, cinema ventures have taken a blow. As a result, film VFX and post-production are likely to suffer as a result. Animation for television and the internet might rebound more quickly.

More and more artists and businesses are considering licencing their content/music to digital platforms in order to make cash. It is critical that the government establishes simple and organised licencing systems and royalty rates so that new content may be easily made accessible for public use and artists can get their fair share of royalties. To maintain public health and safety, individuals all around the world are being forced to change to new everyday habits and routines as a result of the coronavirus pandemic. Many in the entertainment and music industries are concerned about the slowdown in live events and shows. However, there is still work to be done — it may just take a little creative approach.

In our analysis, we have covered how the situation has impacted various media segments like Print, Gaming, OTT, TV, Films and so on in terms of a shift in consumption as per country and generation.

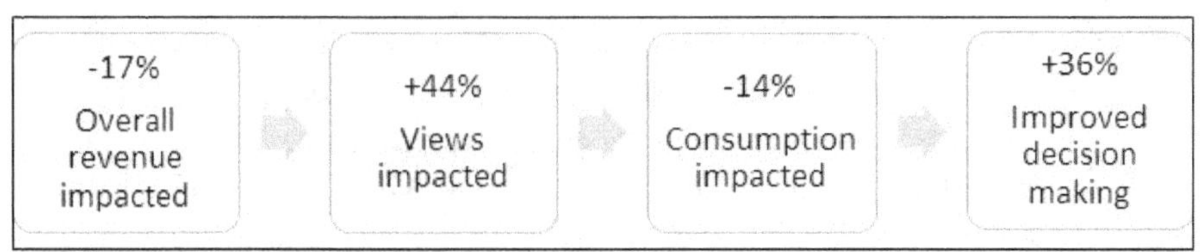

Figure 4 It shows content % based on usage and Expected future trends

Advancements Post Covid: Way Forwards to adapt this trending Media & Entertainment mode

Advancement 1: At this point, the parties should evaluate the agreements for termination and force majeure clauses, as well as determine whether the timetables and duties may be agreed changed. The parties must determine if production schedules and release dates may be postponed in light of staff limitations and audiences' incapacity to attend theatres.

Due to the suspension of movement and prolonged social distancing measures, it is recommended that future agreements be executed via e-agreements and e-stamping. As genuine agreements, e-agreements are subject to stamp duty at the time of execution. The same charge, however, will be imposed in accordance with state regulations. Maharashtra and the National Capital Territory of Delhi, for example, give particular assistance. Both parties can digitally sign the document and have it stamped electronically on the same day in such circumstances.

Advancement 2: It is advised that stakeholders in live entertainment events evaluate ticket terms and conditions, their policies and their duties in respect to delivering services under the appropriate consumer laws to understand their position regarding event cancellations and refunds.

Advancement 3: Because no two insurance contracts are alike, it's crucial to remember that each policy's language is unique, so pay close attention to the exclusions and special endorsements. A number of insurers are establishing unique coronavirus plans or allowing modification of current policies to cover the treatment of the sickness in the event of infected people, and companies should assess them for their workers, customers, or members.

Advancement 4: The film industry is considering restarting production now that the lockdown has been lifted across the country. The problem that the sector is facing is a conflict between the desire to start a business and the necessity to preserve the health and safety of its employees. To guarantee that on-site and off-site filming venues, studios, vanity vans, and other locations are free of the coronavirus, a set of industry guidelines will need to be established. The following are some significant issues to think about:

- Mandating that all employees stay in hotels or assigned housing and isolate themselves from friends and family for the duration of a shoot;
- To provide crew members with masks and gloves;
- Instituting extra cleaning shifts;
- Ensuring that makeup artists and hairdressers have a "one-time-use" strategy for all their tools, including makeup kits, brushes, and so on;
- Limiting the number of people on set at any given moment;
- While filming internationally, ensure safety and health measures as per that country's guidelines.

While properly overseeing production and adhering to all health rules and social distancing measures can assist limit the danger of potential responsibility, there is no assurance that there will be zero risk. The media industry has to switch to this new version of living and providing entertainment to the world in the best suitable manner.

CHAPTER EIGHTEEN

A Critical Analysis of the Impact of Globalization on Indian Education System

**Dr. Archana S. S

Abstract

Globalization is the process of distributing various objects and experiences to people at all corners of the earth. Globalization has a wide-ranging potential to influence all sectors of development. The impact of globalization on education will need both rethinking and restructuring to best prepare the children and the youth of the world to engage globalization's new challenges and opportunities. The present study analyses and explores the impacts of globalization on the Indian education system. The sample selected for the study was 50 teachers working in different colleges of Kerala state. The method adopted was the descriptive survey method. The findings revealed that globalization has significant positive and negative impacts on Indian Education System.

Key Words: Globalization, Internationalization, Information, and Communication Technology, Indian Education System

Introduction

Globalization designates a growth of international exchange and interdependence. It is an elaborate succession of economic, social, technological, cultural and political changes across the globe. Globalization is the space-time compression, it shrinks space as well as time and brings together nation's cultures and economies. It is a phenomenon increasing interdependence and interaction among people, companies and governments of different nations. Globalization is driven by international trade and innovation in information technology. It is the cumulative interconnection of people and places as a consequence of advances in transport, communication, Information Technology, and education.

Globalization refers to the production and distribution of products and services of homogenous types and quality on a worldwide basis. It is expected to have a positive influence on the quantity, quality and spread of knowledge through increased interaction among the various countries (Sachs and Warner, 1995). Its major concern is to deliver world-class education with an updated curriculum and practical acquaintance by attracting talented and experienced persons into academics. Globalization affects upon education in three ways, by admitting foreign students, offering educational programs in foreign campuses through tie-ups or collaborations and establishing educational campuses in foreign countries.

The effect of globalization on education brings rapid developments in technology, communication and knowledge economy. The education system in India before globalization, under innumerable context, hurts from acute scarcity of funds, lack of self -sufficiency and problems of affiliation. Globalization has a multi-dimensional impact on Indian Education. The impact of globalization and the development of a knowledge-based economy have caused much dramatic change to the character and functions of the Indian education system. The major drift is the reforming and restructuring of Indian education to make it more competitive globally. It promotes new tools and techniques in the area like E-learning, blended learning, flexible learning, distance education programs and overseas training. It encouraged the entry of foreign universities in India to set up in collaboration with existing Indian institutions, colleges to promote global research activities for sustainable development. It will also improve Indian educational standards as well as solve the burgeoning problem of enrolment. The influence of foreign education benefited a lot to Indian students to boost their growth at an international level.

Knowledge is the powerful force in the rapidly shifting globalized economy and society (Forbes,2000). The quantity and quality of specialized human resources regulate their competence in the global market. Under the influence of globalization and with the abundance of natural resources, India earned huge young and skilled manpower to excel in every walks of life. Globalization as the driving force, clearly presents new opportunities, challenges and risks for Indian education. Globalization exposed far-reaching implications for socio-economic development and educational systems all over the country. But in order to contribute it to national development, urgent steps will be taken to protect the system from cultural degradation and privatization. Hence, along with the quantitative expansion of education quality must be maintained in relation to the global market.

Need and Significance of the study

Globalization is an international platform for keeping evenness in the living mode of people all over the world. Globalization is the consequence of the exchange of worldly assessments, thoughts and the various aspects of the culture everywhere around the world

(Berman and Machin, 2004). Globalization has emphasized the need for reforms in the educational system with specific reference to the wider application of information technology. The goal of India is to establish a knowledge society in the context of increasing globalization. The impact of globalization on the education system is both positive as well as negative. In order to improve the quality and excellence of Indians through education, it is necessary to analyze globalization in a deeper sense for identifying its positive and negative impact on the Indian Education system. The need and significance of the study are hence justified.

Statement of the problem

Education empowers people with necessary competitive skills and knowledge. It has been appreciated that it is the quality of education that makes one fits for all pursuits of life. Even though globalization upgraded the Indian education system quantitatively and qualitatively it exerts certain pressures on the Indian Education system. The present study analyzed the positive and negative consequences of globalization on the Indian education system. The study is hence entitled '*A Critical Analysis of the Impact of Globalization on Indian Education System*'

Objective

1. To analyze the impact of globalization on the Indian Education System.

2. To identify the positive and negative impacts of globalization on the Indian Education System.

Hypothesis

Globalization has significant positive and negative impacts on Indian Education System

Methodology

Method

The investigator adopted the descriptive survey method for the study as it affords opportunities for

determining the predominant conditions and it is essentially a technique of quantitative description of the characteristics selected for the study. Since the present study aims to analyse the impact of globalization on the Indian Education system, a descriptive survey method was found suitable for the study.

Population

The population of the study involves Teaching faculties from different universities in Kerala state.

Sample

The sample selected for the study involves 50 Teachers working in different Arts and Science Colleges of Thiruvananthapuram, Kollam, Kottayam and Kozhikode districts in Kerala state.

The tool used for the study

The investigator developed a questionnaire consisting of closed and open-ended questions for the faculties to seek views and to analyze the impact of globalization on the Indian Education System. The questionnaire consists of sixteen questions related to eight different facets of globalization on the Indian education system

The procedure adopted for the study

The present study is online-based, due to the existing context of the Covid-19 pandemic. The questionnaire was administered to the sample through a google form. The completed response forms were analysed by using suitable statistical techniques.

Analysis and interpretation

The data collected were analyzed by using a bi-modal approach. The closed-ended questions were analyzed quantitatively by calculating percentages. The qualitative analysis of the open-ended part of the questionnaire were used for collecting the views of teachers associated with the impact of globalization on Indian Education System.

Table 1

No	Factors	Yes		No
		GE (%)	SE (%)	(%)
1.	Improved the quality of Indian Education System	98	2	0
2	Implemented new methods of learning such as e-learning, blended learning etc.	96	2	2
3	Provide opportunities to establish collaboration with Foreign Universities for getting high quality education	92	4	4
4.	Enable students to develop understanding of the culture of foreign countries	94	6	0
5	Literacy rates have improved	86	10	4
6	Encouraged to adopt alternative learning systems such as home schooling, distance education and world schooling	98	2	0
7	Promoted the culture and values of advanced countries	92	6	2
8	Promoted privatization of educational institutions	98	2	0

Analysis of the impact of globalization on the Indian Educational System.

* GE- Great Extent, SE- Some Extent

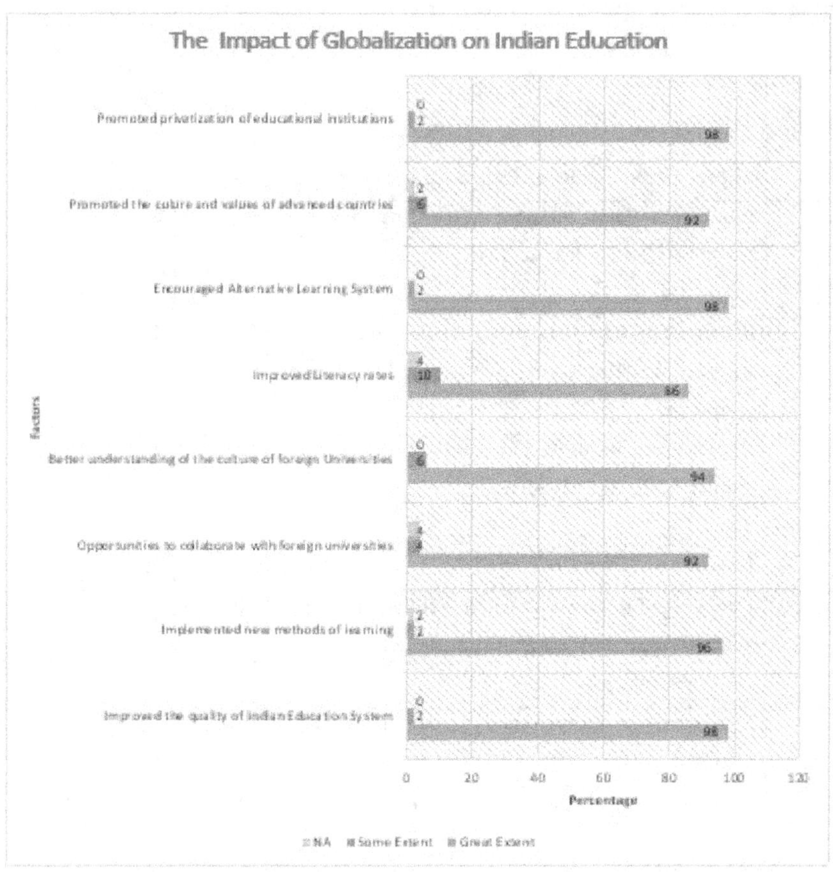

Figure:1 Analysis of the impact of globalization on the Indian Education System.

From Table 1, it is obvious that, out of the total sample {N=50}, the majority (GE-98%) of Teachers opined that globalization improved the quality of the Indian Education System, it encouraged to adopt alternative learning systems in Indian Education and it promoted privatization of educational institutions. 96 % unveiled that globalization implemented new methods of learning such as e-learning and blended learning. The majority of teachers (GE-94%) reported that globalization enabled students to develop an understanding of the culture of foreign countries. Most of the teachers (GE-92%) disclosed that globalization promoted the culture and values of advanced countries in India. 92% of teachers accepted that globalization played a very significant role for getting high-quality education to Indian students by providing opportunities to collaborate with foreign universities. While considering globalization and its impact on improving the literacy rates in India, only 86 % of teachers conveyed it to "Great Extent" at the same time 10% considered it as "Some Extent". Interpretations and explanations of the above-mentioned findings were given below

Positive Impact of Globalization on Indian Educational System

1. Improved the quality of the Indian Education System

Globalization improved the quality of the Indian Education system through *Internationalization*. By promoting healthy competition among countries, it encouraged to exchange of scholars among different countries. It endorsed reputed scholars from various countries to involve in different stages of curriculum designing and transaction of knowledge. Globalization helps students across the world to attain up-to-date information. It provided an opportunity for the teachers and students from different parts of the world to converge and collaborate in educational practices.

1. Implemented New methods of learning

Globalization revolutionized Indian education by implementing new methods of learning such as e-learning and blended learning. It encouraged the teachers to adopt face-to-face or traditional classroom learning with online learning or e-learning. E-learning is learning utilizing electronic technologies to access educational curriculum outside of a traditional classroom Blended learning is a blend of more than one method of delivery. By mixing different modes of delivery teachers can optimize the learning outcome. It is an approach of meeting the challenges of 'Tailor- made' learning and development according to the needs of individuals by integrating innovative technological advances.

3. Provided opportunities to collaborate with foreign universities

Globalization encouraged Universities across the world to search for possibilities by forming a global partnership and fostering relationships with institutions. Universities have a wealth of knowledge and talent, for academic quality improvement and for adopting up-to-date information in educational practices, most of the academics need to work with industry partners, working together can often be a win-win for both parties. These collaborations often deliver truly groundbreaking results in the Indian Education system by promoting foreign education with cost-effective means, global exposure to Indian teachers and students, creating a suitable platform to renovate the Indian education system by taking innovative ideas from foreign countries, getting classes from international faculties and faculty empowerment training from foreign academicians.

4. Promoted the cultural understanding of foreign countries

Among Indian students globalization promoted international understanding, collaboration, harmony and acceptance of cultural diversity across countries and regions by facilitating multiway communication as that of institutional interactions and encouraging multicultural combinations at different levels through education.

5. Improved the literacy rates

Globalization leads India to realize the importance of education and hence literacy rates have improved to meet the challenges and demands.

6. Encouraged alternative learning system

Globalization creates new ideas, values, identities, practices and movements in the Indian education system. In the globalization era, the world is like an independent platform where learners get enough chances for discovering their innate abilities, talents and skills. Globalization demands flexibility, with flexible people in continuous, lifelong learning, it promoted the *Open and Distance Learning (ODL) Universities.* ODL Universities have given access to higher education to those persons who are lacking the formal qualifications to access the traditional Universities. It provides an opportunity to a large number of Indian students who otherwise have been unable to get an education because of geographical distance or the inability to combine traditional studies in work. The ability to produce output that is collaborative in global networks is more appreciated by the market than an academic degree fixed in space and time.

Negative Impact of Globalization on Indian Education System

1. Promoted the culture and values of advanced countries

Globalization potentially creates serious negative impacts on underdeveloped and developing countries like India by rapidly increasing technological gaps and the digital divide between rich areas and poor areas. This leads more opportunities for a few advanced countries and increases inequalities and conflicts between areas and cultures. Further, the advanced countries promote their dominant cultures and values among developing and underdeveloped countries. Globalization exerts a hazardous influence on unique Indian culture.

1. Promoted privatization of educational institutions

Globalization encouraged the participation of the private sector in the field of education. The Indian Education system also witnessed the entry of the private sector on a large scale. The immediate impact of privatization in education is commercialization which makes education very costlier. Privatization primes education accessible to rich people by indirectly avoiding poor and weaker sections of people.

Tenability of Hypothesis

Analysis of the data reveals that Globalization has significant positive and negative impacts on Indian Education System. Hence, the proposed Hypothesis, ***Globalization has significant positive and negative impacts on Indian Education System,*** is accepted.

Major Findings

I. Globalization has had significant impacts on Indian Education System.

II. The positive impacts of globalization on the Indian Education System are

1. Improved the quality of the Indian Education System.
2. Implemented new methods of learning.
3. Provided opportunities to collaborate with foreign Universities.
4. A better understanding of the culture of foreign countries
5. Improved literacy rates

III. The negative impacts of globalization on the Indian Education System are

1. Promoted the culture and values of advanced countries.
2. Promoted privatization of educational institutions.

Conclusion

Globalization is the system of interaction among the countries of the world in order to develop the global economy. Education in global society has the greater responsibility of shaping the preferred future of the students. Liberalization and privatization have changed the education scenario of today. The quantity and quality of education determine the means through which countries can participate in the processes of globalization. The aim of globalization in education is to create global citizens. A global citizen is one who is aware of the wider world, its culture and values diversity, and has a sense of his or her own role as a world citizen.

Reference

- Berman, E. and Machin, S. (2004), Globalization, Skill-Biased Technological Change and Labour Demand, in Lee, E. and M. Vivarelli (eds.), Understanding Globalization, Employment and Poverty Reduction, Palgrave Macmillan, New York, pp. 39-66.
- Forbes, K. J. (2000), 'A Reassessment of the Relationship between Inequality and Growth, *American Economic Review*, vol. 90-4, pp. 869-87
- Lindert, P. and Williamson, J. G. (2001), 'Does Globalization Make the World More Unequal?', *NBER-Working Paper* No. 8228.
- Morrison, C. and Murtin, F. (2007). 'Education Inequalities and the Kuznets Curves: a Global Perspective since 1870' , Paris-Jourdan Working Paper 2007-12.
- O'Rourke, K. and Williamson, J. G. (1999), 'Globalization and History, Cambridge: Cambridge University Press.
- Sachs, J. and Warner, A. (1995), 'Economic Reform and the Process of Global Integration, *Brookings Papers on Economic Activity*, 1995:1, pp. 1-118.
- Steckel, R and Floud, R. (1997) (eds.), 'Health and Welfare During Industrialization', Chicago and London: Chicago Univ. Press.

List Of Authors

1.An analysis on how COVID19 puts women at more risk than men in India

*Dr.Mukta Goyal, Principal, Manvi Institute of Education & Technology, SCERT, New Delhi.

2.Impact of Corona Pandemic on Agricultural Economy in Chhattisgarh

*Chiranjibi Sabar,Asst.Professor(AD-Hoc)Department of Anthropology & Tribal Development, Guru Ghasida Vishwavidyalaya, Bilaspur, Chattisgarh.

**Dinesh Kumar Dahariya, Scholar, Department of Anthropology & Tribal Development, Guru Ghasida Vishwavidyalaya, Bilaspur, Chattisgarh.

3.The Global Epidemic Of Covid – 19 And Its Impact On India

*Swarup Biswas, M.Phil Research Scholar, Department of Political Science, Kazi Nazrul University, Asansol, West Bengal.

4.Covid 19 Pandemic and Indian Tribes

*Krittibas Datta, State Aided College Teacher, Department of Political Science, Jalangi Mahavidyalaya, Murshidabad, West Bengal, India.

5.Covid Vaccine and Curruption

*Dr. Archana Deshpande, Associate Professor, Guru Nanak Institute of Management, Delhi.

**Kanishka Tomar, Pupil-teacher, Manvi Institute of Education And Technology, SCERT

***Souman Debnath, Assistant Professor, Dept. of Political Science, Dwijendralal College, Krishna Nagar, West Bengal.

6.Social Media and Mental Health During the Outbreak of COVID-19

*Sheuli Das, Post Graduate in Education, Rabindra Bharati University, Kolkata, West Bengal.

**Tanvir Ahmed Mondal, Post Graduate in Education, Fakir Chand College, affiliated to the University of Calcutta, Diamond Harbour, West Bengal.

7.Issues and Challenges of COVID 19 on rural economy in West Bengal

*Ratan Shil, M.Phil Scholar, Department of Political Science, University of Kalyani, Kalyani, West Bengal.

8.Global Politics on Covid-19 Vaccine: Changes and Issues

*Sk Abdul Shahid, State Aided College Teacher (SACT-I), Department of Political Science, Chandrakona Vidyasagar Mahavidyalaya, West Bengal.

9.Global Politics and Covid Vaccine

*Tanwangini Sahani, Student, MBA (FA), GGSIPU, Delhi.

**Dr. Abhishek Srivastava, Associate Professor, Faculty of Management Studies, Gopal Narayan Singh University, Rohtas, Bihar.

10.Women, Vaccination, and COVID-19 in India: Challenges & Issues

*Gurpinder Kumar, Assistant Professor, Centre for Women's Studies, University of Allahabad, Prayagraj, UP-211002, INDIA. Email-wsgurpinder@gmail.com

11.The Cursed COVID-19 and its Consequences: A Critical Study.

*Dr. Ratan Chandra Das, State Aided College Teacher (SACT), Dept. of English, Nani Bhattacharya Smarak Mahavidyalaya,, Jaigaon, Alipurduar, West Bengal

12.COVID-19 3rd WAVE

*Dr.Amit Kumar Verma, Department, Faculty of pharmacy, M.J. P. rohelkhand university, Bareli, Uttarpradesh., India.

**Km Jagrati, Scholar of B. Pharma, Faculty of pharmacy, Raja Balwant Singh Engineering Technical Campus Bichpuri, Agra, Uttarpradesh.

***Mrs. Preeti Mishra, Faculty of pharmacy, Raja Balwant Singh Engineering Technical Campus Bichpuri, Agra, Uttarpradesh.

13.Post Pandemic Work-Life Balance Strategies An Empirical Study

*P. Horsley Solomon, Head, Department of Electronics Science, SRM Arts and Science College Kattankulathur - 603 203,Chengalpattu Dist.

**Dr. Alok Tiwari,Assistant Professor,Dept. Of Yogic Science,Dr. Rammanohar Lohia Avadh University, Ayodhya.

14.Degeneration of Education: Impact of Covid-19 on Education

*Debabrata Nandi.SACT in the Department of History, Chandidas Mahavidyalaya

15.COVID 19 CRISIS: PRESENT AND UPCOMING CHALLENGES FOR INDIA

*Jakir Ali Kazi, Independent Scholar, M.A in Political Science, Department of Political Science, University of Gour Banga, Malda, West Bengal.

16.Inequalities and Discrimination around Covid-19 Outbreak

*Sk Abdul Khalid, Independent Researcher, M.A in History, Netaji Subhash Open University, Saltlake, Kolkata

17.Covid Pandemic Crisis On Media & Entertainment Industry

Ms. Nikita Jain, Sr. Assistant Professor, IIMT, Delhi

**Dr. Seema Nath Jain, Associate Professor, IIMT, Delhi*

***Dr. Anshika Rajvanshi, Sr. Assistant Professor, IIMT, Delhi*

18.A Critical Analysis of the Impact of Globalization on the Indian Education System

Dr. Archana S. S, Assistant Professor, mar Theophilus training college, Nalanchira, Thiruvananthapuram, Kerala state.